HOW TO WRITE A BESTSELLER

An Insider's Guide to
Writing Narrative Nonfiction for
General Audiences

Tilar J. Mazzeo

Yale
UNIVERSITY PRESS
NEW HAVEN & LONDON

Published with assistance from the foundation established in
memory of Calvin Chapin of the Class of 1788, Yale College.

Yale University Press books may be purchased in quantity
for educational, business, or promotional use. For information, please
e-mail sales.press@yale.edu (U.S. office) or sales@yaleup.co.uk
(U.K. office).

Printed in the United States of America.

ISBN 978-0-300-26716-7 (paperback)
ISBN 978-0-300-26717-4 (hardcover)

Library of Congress Control Number: 2024930681
A catalogue record for this book is available from the British Library.

10 9 8 7 6 5 4 3 2 1

CONTENTS

HOW TO WRITE A BESTSELLER

INTRODUCTION

The Public-Facing Scholar

Budgets are tight. Enrollments are down. Your dean is asking about impact metrics. Covid-19 and the newly broad familiarity with online content delivery have accelerated painful employment changes already under way in the academy. We hear of departments being closed and faculty teaching positions being eliminated, a forced professional re-tooling. Academic publications wonder aloud about the academy and the Great Resignation. For too many new Ph.D.s, "alt-ac" is a reality rather than a choice.

The formulations are different but the question asked in the popular press, in the halls of legislatures, and increasingly in the faculty lounge is the same: What is the role of the scholar and the expert today? That question leads, inevitably, to others: how do academics reach a wider audience, flourish in an information saturated culture, effect change in policy and culture, and communicate relevance in a moment when the traditional expert is suspect? What it means to be a credible expert is evolving. We live in a culture that values showing over telling, Instagram over pundits.

In an article titled "The Case for Academics as Public Intellectuals," Rick Reis, a Stanford University professor, wrote starkly, and somewhat scoldingly: "Academics no longer possess the privilege . . . of choosing to remain cloistered within the walls of the academy, engaging only with members of their disciplines." And, in fact, the classroom is increasingly seen as a public space, and online Zoom meetings are not the only reason. Legislation already allows for recording lectures in the classrooms of public universities without the consent of the faculty, and professors are public figures whether they position themselves in that way or not. History tells us that global crises reshape institutions and accelerate structural change. That is likely to be the case in the academy.

In the midst of every crisis there is also opportunity, and certainly in the case of academics writing for general audiences this is true. There are abundant opportunities at our current crossroads. Funding bodies have been, perhaps unusually, at the forefront of one new direction in the academy (and of one new direction for researchers looking for alt-academic avenues). The Mellon Foundation now offers fellowships to doctoral students making the transition to writing and researching for broader audiences (www.humanitiesforall.org). The National Endowment for the Humanities has committed $1.7 million in support for "researchers who want to write books in a style other than the traditional academic monograph" (www.neh.gov/grants/research/public-scholar-program). Both programs remain vibrant and important. Perhaps the biggest opportunity of all is this: publishers, both trade houses and university presses, want to publish books by academics who can demonstrate that they are able to write for a broad, general audience.

The stumbling block is simply this: how?

How does a career academic get started? Indeed, how does anyone with high-quality research skills and an area of fact-based expertise, either academic or industry, find a point of entry into a broad audience market? What does that transition look like, both at the level of project conceptualization and at the level of writing? How does one navigate this crossroads in the academic institution? How do we navigate, as well, a new, business-oriented professional culture? Perhaps most important, in how we communicate with our publishers, editors, chairs, and deans: how do we connect for ourselves, as scholars, the places where public writing and the public sphere in which modern democracies were created and are sustained—that *res publica* that is at the heart of relevance—touch in ways that are rich and sustaining for readers and for us as writers?

This book focuses on answering one pragmatic and practical question: how, at the level of the "nitty-gritty" doing-of-the-thing, does one write successfully for general audiences? It is a short, personal, and somewhat polemical guide. It is positioned somewhere between a how-to book and a treatise, and if it is at times unsparingly blunt in its opinions and recommendations, it is based on fifteen years of direct experience as an academic who made the jump to writing multiple *New York Times, Los Angeles Times,* and *San Francisco Chronicle* bestsellers. It is also written from the background of someone trained, in her academic capacity, in the study of narrative.

How did I make that jump? I won't pretend that it was easy or that luck didn't play a role in it. But it also took skill and time to make this transition.

My story is the story of an academic who, depending on your perspective, either made the jump to writing for general audiences or went off the career rails sometime circa 2007. I was trained as a doctoral student in English and comparative literature in the 1990s, with a specialization in narrative and cultural theories. I was among the very fortunate new Ph.D.s in the late 1990s to land quickly on the tenure track, working at two large state universities before moving to a highly selective liberal arts college in New England. At that liberal arts college, I earned tenure and then an endowed chair and served a brief tour of duty as a department chair. I view the peculiar culture of the academy, in short, as an insider. I have chaired hiring searches and tenure decisions, I have reviewed contingent faculty contracts, and I have been, as part of a transcontinental and later international "two-body problem," a frequent flier on the job market, off and on, for more than two decades. That experience on the job market has included having to position titles written for a general audience on a curriculum vitae in a profession in which writing in this way is not yet fully integrated or normalized.

I can speak, as not many in our profession can, directly to the special issue of what it means to consider writing for general audiences prior to tenure. I have only understood how unusual it is — and how lucky I was — in retrospect.

I published my first scholarly monograph on the academic list at the University of Pennsylvania Press in 2006, six years after receiving my doctorate: right on time by the mores of the profession. Around that same time, I found myself chatting with a friend from graduate school, a historian who was moving away from the tenure track trajectory and who had published her first book with a commercial press and on a trade list. For a publisher, whether it is a university press or a commercial house, books on the "trade list" are distinct from those on the "academic list," and the fundamental difference is that, for trade publications, book sales matter.

I had the idea for a second book, an idea well suited for a general audience but still within my field. My friend suggested that I write a nonfiction trade book proposal and send it off to an agent. On a whim — and emboldened largely because I simply did not know any better — I wrote a draft proposal, intending to do just that. When I sent it to my friend, she returned it covered with red ink. She tried to explain to me what I was doing wrong. My writing, she said, was just "too academic."

I still had very little idea what that meant, but based on her feedback and edits, I was able to put together a book proposal that was a convincing bluff. I sent it to my academic editor, who said that he could offer a modest advance to place the book on their trade list but encouraged me to take it instead to an agent and a commercial press. Within weeks, I had an agent and a book contract from one of the "Big Five" publishers that dominate most of the commercial book market, with an advance that was equal to my annual salary as an assistant professor.

That timeline and experience is atypical. A period of months is more common than weeks, and generally it takes a few tries to land on a topic and find an agent, even with a solid book proposal. At the same time, that is my story, and I think there is a value in my speaking bluntly and truthfully, academic to academic, about what this can look like and how you, too, can achieve it.

Had that contract come just as I was slated to begin a semester of teaching, what followed also might have been different. I had the immense privilege of one academic monograph in press and an upcoming year-long pre-tenure sabbatical to complete this new project, and so I found myself very quickly — before I had time to second guess the wisdom of what I was doing — out of the frying pan and deep into the fire.

Writing that first book meant for a general audience was not easy. In fact, it was agonizing. After I wrote the first third of the manuscript, I sent it to my editor, and she invited me to a champagne lunch on the Embarcadero in San Francisco, near where we were both located that autumn. All I can say to you is that when your editor wants to deliver good news, she does not do it over champagne. She broke the news to me in person that the book was not working. I still remember her words: "It's too academic." She was a lovely person and could not have been kinder, but I cried the entire drive home, and I was racked by all kinds of self-doubt in the weeks and months that followed. I finally picked myself up and rewrote the entire first third a second time from scratch.

And, a second time, we had a champagne lunch in San Francisco.

It was only on the third attempt at writing the first third of *The Widow Clicquot* from the ground up that I was told, yes, this book could become a bestseller. And in fact, the book hit the *New York Times* nonfiction bestseller list in the month or so after publication. We ultimately made the *San Francisco Chronicle* bestseller list and bestseller lists in Australia. The book has been translated into a dozen or so foreign languages. It was reviewed in the *New York Times* and the *Wall Street Journal*. As I write the final manuscript for this book, filming has just finished on a major motion picture adaptation, and to this day I continue to receive royalties on the sales of the title.

Since that time, I have published six more nonfiction books for general audiences, including one other *New York Times* bestseller and a *Los Angeles Times* bestseller, have had two other books optioned for film, and been interviewed on NPR, BBC, RTL, and CBC radio and television. I've received a snarky review in the *Guardian* and a charming write-up in *Le Figaro*. And, perhaps in spite of having published a "popular" book, I did get tenure. In the end, however, for reasons also connected to trade writing, I also walked away from a tenured professorship and an endowed chair in my late forties, in part because over time the fit became less tenable.

Different people get to different places through different avenues. I am not claiming that my way is the only path on this journey. I do claim this as familiar terrain, however, and this book is my very candid advice for what I would do (and not do), knowing what I know now, if I were looking to write for the first time a trade nonfiction book as a public-facing scholar or researcher. There is some frank advice on such matters as contingent appointments, the tenure track, the job market, cranky colleagues, recalcitrant deans, and unsupportive senior administrators. I talk about agents and social media and the basics of contracts, advances, delivery, and the vexing matter of footnotes and endnotes.

Primarily, though, this book focuses on three things: the readiness that making this transition requires; the pragmatics of finding, structuring, and selling a general audience topic and book proposal; and concrete examples of how we move from writing that is "too academic" to "bestseller quality" while continuing to work as a scholar and fact-based expert.

How to begin? That readiness is crucially important. I work on a regular basis as a developmental editor with people looking to write trade nonfiction. Most of those people, by dint of my particular background, happen to be academics. In the past fifteen years, I have had many academics tell me that they want to write "popular" nonfiction.

I have seen some of those colleagues succeed in making the transition. I have also seen colleagues fail.

The colleagues who have been able to transition to writing for general audiences all had one thing in common: they were able to adopt (and to keep) what a Buddhist might call a beginner's mind, what scientists studying neuroplasticity call a growth mind-set, and what I generally just refer to as an ability to bounce back from tough champagne lunches.

Those who succeeded ended up being good general audience writers. They didn't all start there. But what they all had in common was a willingness to begin at the beginning and not to get it right the first time — or even the second time.

The colleagues who have failed to make the transition to writing for general audiences struggled for different and diverse reasons, but I have seen a consistent predictive pattern: those colleagues who ultimately did not succeed were those who became frustrated and defensive easily. They could not bounce back after negative feedback. I have only rarely seen one of these colleagues get beyond the topic stage. That's perhaps to be expected: the transition from an academic topic to a general audience topic is a fair bit harder than the sentence-level transition from academic writing to trade writing, probably because the shift is almost entirely a change of mind-set.

Why do these smart people get so knee-jerk defensive and find themselves unable to hold open the space needed to learn something they are curious about doing? I have my theories. I suspect that we could write a whole (other) book on how the structure of the academy cultivates defensiveness as an adaptive strategy, but experience has taught me that it's generally fatal to writing for a general audience. And that's because a lot of the defensiveness masks a certain ambivalence about that audience.

We might as well just speak the truth plainly: there are people in the academy who believe that writing a book for general audiences is dumbing down your research. There are people who believe that your average reader is not capable of understanding expert concepts. It is hard not to internalize some of this as you embark on writing your book. You will have colleagues and senior administrators who believe that general audience work is not "real" research or is, at best, research that is of lower value. While this is not universal, I do know of merit-review committees where bestselling history books have been wholesale excluded as research for salary and promotion. It is entirely likely that, in the actual mechanics of promotion and tenure, should you be among those favored few fortunate enough to occupy a permanent academic post and be eligible for promotion and tenure, your general audience work will be relatively devalued, and I discuss further on what I think this means for contingent, alt-academic, and pre-tenure academic colleagues.

If you are successful enough as a general audience author, I can also almost guarantee you that sooner or later you will have someone inside the academy tell you that you are a hack or a sellout. And, of course, the push toward royalty-free open-access publication is fundamentally at odds with writing trade nonfiction. This poses a particular institutional hurdle for British colleagues especially. Both open-access publication and trade publication are models that share the goal of making research more accessible to the public, but they take very different approaches to intellectual property and labor. I have heard voiced the complaint that writing for trade is too capitalist, despite the fact that open-access publishing conglomerates like Elsevier make scandalous profits that most trade presses could only dream about. (If you're curious to learn more, I recommend Martin Hagve's article "The Money Behind Academic Publishing," published in 2020 in *Tidsskriftet,* as a good eye-opener.)

I would (and will) argue that none of these things about the intellectual inferiority of trade writing are true. But they are truisms, and they are part of the terrain that academics making the transition to writing for general audiences are navigating. As academics, we are trained to approach information and problems in highly specialized ways. Those ways mostly have their origins in the Enlightenment and in a particular set of institutional and cultural values that prioritize objectivity, deductive reasoning, empiricism, and narrow expertise. These are highly effective intellectual skills, and writing for general audiences does not mean disavowing them. However, there are other ways of communicating expertise. Writing well for general audiences does require a willingness to think beyond our academic training and institutional culture.

Let's put one other thing on the table as well: as academics, we are acculturated to define ourselves by our specialization. We tend to be workaholics and to be especially work-identified. We tend to be high achievers. After all, we would not have ended up where we are if we weren't the kids who got A's. It is hard in the academy not to conflate our personal worth as people with our expertise in our subject matter. This fact also makes redefining our topic into something more popular particularly loaded.

Here is a scenario I've seen many times. An academic wants to write a so-called "popular" book and proposes some aspect of his research field that he finds deeply compelling and worth sharing. The response he gets is that the proposed general audience topic is not sufficiently interesting, not marketable, not timely, not broad enough, not "big" enough, too narrow. What the person telling the academic author this means is simply: this is not a general audience topic. What the academic hears is: *you* are not interesting, you are not marketable, you are outdated, washed up, narrow. This is often made worse, unintentionally, by the fact that the "market" in the academy is the subject of such collective trauma that it is especially hard for academics to hear that they are not marketable.

What goes wrong is that redefining a book topic to be more broadly appealing gets tangled with our work-identified self-perceptions. What usually follows is a reversion to the truisms. Something along the lines of, well, if that's what it means to write a general audience book, then I don't want to dumb down my research like that. To me, that's frustration and defensiveness talking.

So, before you begin, sit yourself down and ask yourself if you're in a mental place where you can bracket what you know and what you've learned about knowing and can come at that knowledge from a different perspective. It's not easy. But finding a general audience topic isn't a referendum on our specialization or expertise. It's about learning to see your specialization and expertise afresh, from the beginner's perspective, where there are lots of options. Writing for general audiences requires practice. Practice requires learning from failure. That's why I began by telling you about champagne lunches. You have to expect a couple of them on your journey to writing a successful trade book.

Chapter 1

THE GENERAL AUDIENCE TOPIC

We need, in order to begin, to have some shared understanding of what writing that is too academic looks like if we're going to talk about how we begin writing for a non-academic general audience. We need to have some shared understanding of what a too-small book topic looks like, and we need to understand the economics and protocols of the world we're entering into, so we don't start wrong end around, which for academics is a common pitfall. So let's see if in this chapter we can set the stage a bit, with the caveat that we'll circle back in the chapters and sections that follow to all these topics in more substantial and nuanced detail.

In broad, sweeping strokes, here's the picture: writing general audience nonfiction means writing for trade. Commercial press, academic press with a trade list: it doesn't really matter. Trade just means writing for book sales and with the hope and expectation of profitability. If there is a big enough audience and the book is good, in theory, there will be buyers. "Big" means sales in the tens of thousands of copies. "Big" does not mean five hundred copies sold to libraries. "Good" means a lot of things. It means well written. For trade nonfiction that generally means narrative and character. It means timely. It means relevant. It means it takes a big idea and makes it a big story. Bigness is measured in sales of books.

What follows from this picture are a few things.

First, you are not going to get a trade publisher to offer you a contract on a book topic that is not likely to appeal to thousands of readers, probably tens of thousands of readers, based on market comparatives.

Second, you are not going to get a trade publisher to offer you a contract for a trade book unless the publisher is confident that you can deliver on the topic with good trade writing.

Third, you are not going to get a trade publisher to offer you a contract for a trade book unless your topic has some kind of compelling narrative arc, brings some fresh and compelling cultural angle, or tells one hell of a story.

Idea, writing, story. All big.

Fourth, and here finally is some nice news, a trade publisher does not need (or want) to see your entire book manuscript before deciding if you have a trade topic and are a good trade writer with a good story. They don't actually want to talk to you at all in the beginning directly. They want a book proposal and, because there are "big" trade publishers and "small" trade publishers, if you're talking to a big trade publisher, they're actually talking to your agent. What your ability to get a contract will depend upon is a book proposal.

What about agents? Everyone always wants to know about agents, so we might as well talk about them up front (and we'll talk a lot more about them later as well). Do you need to schmooze to get an agent? No. Most agents work on commission, in whole or in part. They don't take on authors or titles unless they think a book has sales potential. You won't get an agent for your project if it's too

---

small, if you can't write a strong trade narrative, if you don't have story, no matter how frantically you network at the MLA, because agents aren't going to represent projects that aren't marketable. Marketable books, especially big books written by good writers with great proposals? Agents are going to be delighted to represent those.

Idea, writing, story. All big. All in a book proposal. That's the nut of it.

A book proposal is a genre with relatively fixed rules, and we'll go through the process of developing a strong one. It has a number of fixed sections (though the terms can vary). Inside the industry, the terms you'll normally hear are: narrative summary (idea), comps (market of readers and sales), chapter summaries (story arc), sample chapter (writing), and author platform and marketing (reaching the market). You write the book proposal, get the agent, pitch the editor, get the contract. Only once the ink is dried are you going to start writing that manuscript. That's the process.

It all starts with the idea, and that's inevitably where you need to begin your process. What makes a trade topic? How do you find or generate one? How do you move toward "bigness" of idea? How do you move from your academic area (which is an important part of that author platform) to a general audience book idea? Let's start just with a list. You're looking for an idea that ticks as many of these boxes as possible. Not every successful general audience topic will have every one of those attributes. However, successful general audience titles will have most of these qualities.

First, general audience books are timely. This doesn't mean that the topics need to be contemporary. But they do need to have contemporary relevance. The Cambridge University science historian Seb Falk's *The Light Ages: The Surprising Story of Medieval Science*

(2020) by the summer of 2023 had sold almost eleven thousand copies and been reviewed everywhere from the *Wall Street Journal* to *Smithsonian Magazine*. Medieval science is not obviously a current topic. However, Falk found a timely approach. As the *Financial Times* noted in one of the reviews (February 12, 2021), "*The Light Ages* . . . illuminates not just the visionaries of the past but also the troubled state of anti-intellectualism in the modern world." It speaks to something that many of us have on our mind. It performs the cultural work of helping us think through a current topic. It's timely.

How do you make your topic timely? Start with trying to see your book from the perspective of the audience. Your reader wants the answer to a simple question: So what? Your area of interest is medieval monks. So what? Why does the topic matter now? Who cares and why? What's the big-picture takeaway? How does your topic participate in an ongoing cultural conversation? What is the relevance? "The history of medieval science helps us understand the origins of modern anti-intellectualism" is a great answer. That's a general audience topic and timely. You should be able to answer this question in a single sentence. In fact, a good exercise is to imagine that you are writing that future book review of your title: this book illuminates not only [A] but also [relevant, timely B].

I've found that it's helpful to have an imaginary reader in mind when I'm trying to answer this question. During the decades that I have been part of an academic two-body problem and was commuting bi-coastally, I would work through general audience topics on long-haul flights, by trying to imagine what book topic would interest one or another of my fellow passengers. Why would the executive in 1C want to read that book? Why would the flight crew? How about the young couple holding hands by the galley? You can do the same in any public space that's not your university campus. We write

—

as academics all the time for an imagined audience — the imagined audience of our peers and peer reviewers. Make sure that when you are answering the question "So what?" you are answering it for a general audience reader.

Second, general audience titles move from narrow to broad. A timely topic, relevant to a broad audience, is step one. Now, think about how to broaden that appeal and structure the topic. Later in this book, I am going to encourage you to throw out the idea of the expository thesis entirely and think about writing persuasively using a narrative model. I think there are good communication reasons to do this, good market reasons to do this, and I also think that the expository thesis, precisely because it is so habituated, holds some particular risks for academics looking to write trade nonfiction. It is very easy to fall back into patterns that read as too academic.

For the moment, let's just say that, while some trade nonfiction books may be argument driven, most bestselling trade nonfiction books do not use argument as the only organizing structure or even the main organizing structure, and thesis in a general audience title is developed differently. If your project is being imagined as primarily argument focused, at this stage of development you need, at the very least, to think about the structure of your thesis from a different direction: otherwise, you will end up with an academic topic and not a general audience project.

So let's at least agree to think about argument differently for trade. We all have our own vocabulary for talking about and teaching argument. Because my academic career largely played out at a liberal arts college, I taught English composition every autumn for the better part of twenty years. That means I've spent a lot of time trying to articulate different kinds of theses for different disciplines. If my academic colleagues will forgive the reversion to the terminology of freshman composition, academic audience books and general audience books formulate thesis statements that work in different directions.

I use the language of observational claims and interpretive claims. An expository thesis starts with an arguable truth claim, which is usually an observational claim: something does something. It's followed by a first-order interpretive claim: in order to do or because of something. That is followed by a second-order interpretive claim, which answers the question: and this is important because? Another way to frame timeliness is to think of it as a second-order interpretive claim that makes a statement about a contemporary issue.

To my mind, all theses, if they are fully developed, have all three of these claims articulated, and that's true whether it's for an academic or a general audience. The difference is scope. If academic arguments are microscopes, moving from disciplinary to increasingly specialized sub-field claims, then general audience books are telescopes, moving from a limited set of claims to broad relevance.

In academic-oriented monographs or articles, the direction, moving from largest and broadest to smallest and most narrow, would look something like this: observational claim → first-order interpretive claim → second-order interpretive claim.

Not sure what that means in practice? Let's take, for example, a peer-reviewed article published in a scientific journal. Our sample article's title is "Co-Morbidity of PTSD and Immune System Dysfunction: Opportunities for Treatment," co-authored by Drs. Gretchen Neigh and Fariya Ali and published in *Current Opinions in Pharmacology* in August 2016 (29:104–110). The article is high-quality published research and is organized according to what I would see as the conventions of academic writing; its focus moves toward increased specialization of claims.

The article is reporting on research into the somatic manifestations of post-traumatic stress. It begins with the observation (observational claim: something does something) that "somatic autoimmune and inflammatory diseases and disorders have a high rate of co-morbidity with PTSD." That co-morbidity, the study argues, is not coincidental but organically related: patients with PTSD show "alterations in several primary pathways involving the neuroendocrine and immune systems" especially in relation to the HPA axis, GC signaling, and inflammatory responses (first-order claim: in order to/because of something). Therefore, given the limited effectiveness of direct GR and HPA axis interventions, the clinical recommendation (second-order claim: this is important because) is to focus on immuno-centric approaches, senolytics, and SSRI pharmaceuticals.

The academic topic moves, quite naturally, toward specialization. I am an English professor by training. I know what inflammatory disease and co-morbidity mean. I have only a very imprecise idea, however, what senolytics are or what a GR and HPA axis does, precisely because the interpretive claims are meant for a highly specialized audience of researchers of which I am not reasonably expected to be a participant.

A general audience book on that same topic, however, would move in the other direction: The smallest, most narrow, specialized claim would be the observational claim. A bit broader would be the first-order claim. And the broadest and most expansive claim would be the second-order interpretive claim — the "so-what" factor.

Take that same topic: trauma as a somatic disease. Research has demonstrated that the brain has considerable neuroplasticity and that there are neurological pathways related to inflammation and immune response that are implicated in PTSD (observational claim).

Psychological interventions can leverage the brain's neuroplasticity to alter the affected pathways (first-order). If you have experienced trauma (and what human hasn't?), tools such as neurofeedback, meditation, theater, play, or yoga can be effective in improving your life and your health (second-order). That is a general audience thesis. It moves from narrow to broad. It also happens to be the thesis of a number 1 *New York Times* bestselling book, *The Body Keeps the Score,* by Dr. Bessel van der Kolk.

Both pieces of writing are based on expertise and academic research. Dr. van der Kolk is not dumbing down his research by making it relevant to a broad group of people and — importantly — to a broad group of book buyers. The difference is not in the quality of the research or in the quality of the researcher. The difference is that *The Body Keeps the Score* creates timeliness and relevance, and it does that, in part, by turning the thesis to shift the direction of the claims.

If you are going to structure your general audience topic around argument, consider how to redirect the claims. How you do this for your field and your research will be highly specific, but I think there are a couple of things to keep in mind while working through that process.

The first is that you probably need to be prepared to think laterally and to think about moving your claims quite substantially outward. It is very unlikely that your precise area of current research is going to map directly onto a general interest topic, for the simple reason that your current academic research is precisely that: academic oriented.

The second thing is that you may need to be prepared to stretch your definition of your field. We tend as academics to have quite narrow areas of primary expertise, particularly if we are mid-career or later. For a long time in the academy, the advice has been to choose one thing and to be the foremost expert in the world on that thing, and that probably remains wise career advice to anyone pre-tenure especially. In reality, however, you actually do have an expertise that is much broader already than your sub-specialization. Most of us pass comprehensive examinations in areas of knowledge that we never work in again, despite the fact that we possess doctoral level expertise in multiple fields — and the knowledge of how to gain new expertise in new areas.

The wider you can take the lens, the more opportunities you will find for topics. Indeed, one of the things I have most appreciated about writing for general audiences was the freedom to follow my intellectual curiosity into new areas at mid-career, a time when many of us experience boredom and burnout.

The third item on our list of what makes a good general audience topic: general audience books are exposed to cultural and book-publishing trends. Because relevance and timeliness matter, this does mean that general audience books can be somewhat more exposed to cultural fashions. There are certain questions that have an urgency now — anti-intellectualism, inequality — that they did not have, perhaps, a decade ago. *The Body Keeps the Score* was a smart topic and benefited hugely, if belatedly, from precisely this kind of timing. Although it was originally published in 2014 and well reviewed at the time, the book hit the *New York Times* bestseller list in the winter of 2021, a moment when psychological trauma was in the public consciousness.

In October 2021, the publishing industry outlet "Book Riot" published an article for those in marketing and acquisitions asking "Why Is *The Body Keeps the Score* So Popular Right Now?" and their answer was pretty straightforward:

You can map current events in the world pretty well onto the best-sellers list. . . . As COVID-19 spread in early 2020, *The Great Influenza* spent a few weeks at the #1 spot. Then, when George Floyd was murdered and the Black Lives Matter movement gained increased attention, *So You Want to Talk About Race* and *White Fragility* dominated the list for much of the rest of 2020. . . . *The Body Keeps the Score* is, in my opinion, another book that taps into larger current events and conversations. It speaks to the increased recognition of trauma, both the pandemic as a collective trauma and the heightened awareness for other forms of trauma, like sexual trauma and racial trauma as the #MeToo and Black Lives Matter movements have respectively highlighted.

I think this is a pretty fair statement about current events and best-seller lists. It's not that a general audience book has to speak to the current news cycle. In fact, because of the long lead time in book publishing, trying to write a book that will map onto the current news cycle a year or two from now is a lot like trying to catch a falling knife and time the stock market. On the other hand, there are clearly broad cultural trends that occur in cycles of five or ten years, and if you can speak to the relevance and timeliness of your topic in relation to those medium-term trends, you will find a larger audience, have a better chance of reaching book buyers, and have a better chance of having your book published as a general audience title. If you are writing a book on a topic that is misaligned with the news cycle, on the other hand, you may find it particularly tough going.

You will also find publishing a general audience book easier or more difficult depending on market saturation. It does need to be said that writing for a general audience is not a non-profit project on the part of publishers, and that is as true for university presses with trade lists as it is for commercial publishers. As academics, we are sometimes not fully aware of this market reality, because the academic side of academic presses typically are non-profit organizations, where the question an editor asks is not "how much will this book make" but "how much will this book lose."

As we have said, book sales matter in trade publishing. I discuss the economics of publishing in some detail later because it helps to understand, for example, why a trade-list publisher very much wants you to write a nonfiction book that is around eighty or ninety thousand words long and why a publisher is likely not going to accept your four hundred thousand word manuscript for publication. For the moment, just keep in mind that, if there have been a lot of trade books in the general area in which your proposed book falls, a publisher is likely to see the market as saturated unless you can make some persuasive claim that you have something new and noteworthy to offer. Otherwise, the readers interested in that topic are likely to have already purchased enough books to satisfy their curiosity for this decade. The cultural cycle is probably on the downswing. The timeliness and relevance are waning. Book sales are likely to decrease in that area. All of those are factors that make it harder to publish a general audience book when there is perceived market saturation.

Fourth, general audience books are (gently) contrarian. If it's all about book sales and there is no such thing as bad publicity, is it a good idea to write a controversial book? Jordan Peterson, professor emeritus at the University of Toronto, has taken this route as an academic, and he certainly has sold books in the process. Jordan Peterson's notoriety-driven sales numbers aside, I would offer some urgent caveats. For one thing, I don't think it's true that there is no such thing as bad publicity, especially if you are trying to straddle an academic career and a career (or side gig) publishing for a general audience.

Many successful general audience titles do take a contrarian turn and promise to tell us something we don't know on a topic about which we think we're already informed. You'll see language like "untold story" or "hidden danger" or "behind-the-scenes look" in book marketing copy. In general, we probably can add "contrarian" to our list of qualities that are desirable in a general audience topic. I was recently asked this question directly by a publicist: could I highlight for the marketing team the "never-before-told" features of this story? There is a whole section, as well, of the standard nonfiction book proposal — the "comps," or comparatives — that essentially asks prospective authors to answer this question (as well as the question about market saturation).

Contrarian positioning, however, can be gently or highly polemical. My advice, for a whole series of reasons, is to stick to the gently polemical side of that spectrum unless you have some very strong reason for taking a divisive or inflammatory position. For one thing, publishing a general audience book, if it's successful and reaches a large audience, places the author in the public eye in a way that most of us working inside the academy have not experienced. Anyone who spends any time on social media will have seen this dynamic. The public sphere in our day and age is a pretty rough-and-tumble place, and if your goal was to create a controversy, well, don't be surprised if the controversy comes to you.

Perhaps more important, I happen to believe and hope you do as well in the value of the public sphere and its connection to the life of a democracy. Academics have an important role to play in the "public thing" — the "res publica" of a republic — and that does not include throwing intellectual hand grenades into the public sphere. My sense is that most of my academic colleagues also take a dim view of this. There remains in the academy a general consensus that academics are meant to provide balanced approaches to their areas of expertise, and, just as a practical matter, it's not a good plan to burn your academic reputation. It won't help you in the department meetings, but it also won't help you in the long run with your book sales either. My sense is this is a clear example of a lose-lose proposition. Obviously, this is not to suggest that you shy away from the truth if your research leads you to a foundational place. However, there's no purchase in manufacturing unnecessarily controversial claims either.

Finally, general audience book publishing is all about book sales and reaching a broad sector of readers. Although it is true that a highly polemical book can garner a great deal of attention, especially on social media or in partisan news outlets (and especially in opposing partisan news outlets), it is less clear that, in our highly divisive cultural moment, any of this translates into increased book sales. There is good research showing that the posts most likely to be shared or commented on in social media are those to which the user has the strongest negative emotional reaction. A multi-authored cognitive-science study in 2021, for example, published in the *Proceedings of the National Academy of Sciences,* takes the titular position that "Out-Group Animosity Drives Engagement on Social Media" (118:26, e2024292118).

There is a bottom line in the publishing industry, and what matters is not impact or reach (factors that can and do matter in academics), but sales. Are you willing to pay money to buy the book of and reward financially a writer whose views you find obnoxious? Many book buyers are not. Those same readers, however, are apparently happy to retweet furious media coverage of that same controversial title. Don't confuse media exposure and furious tweets with book sales. If impact and reach drive sales, great. But it is possible to overplay this hand such that those become decoupled.

Sixth, general audience titles are unified. "Unified" and "tight" are words that you'll hear in the publishing industry, especially in the general audience sector. What they mean is that the title has a strong internal and organic coherence. We are going to discuss this in greater detail further on, but for the moment let's just say this: there are a couple of different ways that you can unify a general audience book. You can use a big idea as a unifying structure and rely on that public-facing thesis. You can unify through character. You can unify by turning the author into a character. You can unify through narrative. Most of the best general audience books use two or more of those techniques.

Let's take again the example of the mainstream media reviews of Falk's *Light Ages,* where I think the reviews communicate fairly effectively how the book was marketed to a general audience readership and what those readers appreciated about it. The *Wall Street Journal,* November 20, 2020: Falk lets "us inhabit, for a spell of seven finely crafted chapters, the vibrant mind of a 14th-century Benedictine monk." Unified through character. Or the book is "Mr. Falk's own clever astrolabe." Unified through narrative structure. The *Guardian,* September 25, 2020: "as seen through the eyes of a pioneering astronomer." Unified through character. *Forbes,* May 12, 2021: "Falk frames his story around the possible career of . . . John Westwyk." Unified through character. The *Christian Science Monitor,* December 18, 2020: "Falk is a marvelous guide." Unified through author as character.

All right, so you're looking not only for a timely and a gently contrarian topic, of potential interest to a large number of readers, moving outward toward cultural relevance, but also for a unified topic. What does that mean at this stage?

Well, think about academic monographs. These are works in which a certain degree of discontinuity is anticipated. The fact that we have unspoken rules about how many chapters in a book that you can publish as free-standing journal articles before a publisher won't accept the monograph speaks to this. The academic book market in the humanities particularly has moved, for its own economic reasons, away from the single-author monograph. We expect, as a kind of convention of the genre, that academic books, still the gold standard in the humanities and the social sciences, are composite. In the institution where I earned tenure, the minimum guideline was (and I believe remains) five articles placed in top journals or an academic monograph, in tacit acknowledgment that the two were structurally understood to be connected. In the sciences, where co-authored peer-reviewed articles and first-author recognition are the gold standard, the idea of the author's personal voice as a unifying or structuring device in an academic publication is foreign.

General audience books, however, are not five article ideas collected into a single topic, even if those five article ideas were all somehow timely. They rarely have multiple authors. You are looking, instead, for a self-contained topic, where the boundaries are — or will appear to be once you unify it — organic. Falk's astrolabe. The past-present-future structure of David Sinclair and Matthew LaPlante's bestselling "big science" (and, notice, gently contrarian) title on genetics, *Lifespan: Why We Age — and Why We Don't Have To* (Atria, 2019). What Eleanor Cummings writing for the *Atlantic's* issue of October 18, 2021, describes as the "reliable arc" of *The Body Keeps the Score,* centered on illustrative "stories of trauma survivors . . . concluding with a few chapters of actionable advice for individual readers." The eponymous missing diary of Benjamin Franklin's sister, which structures Jill Lepore's *Book of Ages: The Life and Opinions of Jane Franklin* (Vintage, 2014).

We will talk in detail about all these structuring devices, and others, in later chapters, but at the beginning, because you need both a topic and a structuring device that will reach a general audience, think not only about your subject but also about your angle—how you will come to that subject and what the boundaries of your book will be. The academic impulse tends to be encyclopedic: we want to fit into this book everything we know or have discovered about a topic. Dissertations train us to do this. Monographs allow for it. General audience books, however, because the "how" of the communication matters as much as the "what" of the communication, benefit from a more narrowly delineated arena.

Think back to our telescope metaphor earlier: general audience books move from a narrow, fixed point (the observational and first-order claims) and aim to connect those claims to a broad, more universal perspective (second-order claims). But if the distant star we're aiming for is, say, Falk's "troubled state of anti-intellectualism in the modern world" and how that is connected to medieval monasticism in Britain, it is not going to be unifying to throw in a chapter on anti-monasticism in ancient Sumatra. The more successful strategy for general audience titles is to keep a quite tight focus once you've established the topic—tighter than you might for an academic book on the same general topic.

We will discuss the pragmatic elements in considerable detail as we go on, but there are, in fact, a relatively limited number of ways in which narratives are understood to be unified in the Western tradition. Most of our ideas about narrative unity in the Anglophone world have their origins, in particular, in Aristotle, who proposed three of them: unity of action (one principal action), unity of time (one day), or unity of place (one location).

I'm not suggesting that authors need to adopt all three of these unities and certainly not simultaneously. I'm not suggesting we need to follow Aristotle to the letter. I think for one day we could use any clearly delineated time period. For one location, we could reasonably substitute one topic. However, in general, I do think that, if you start looking at books that are considered culturally effective — and good reviews plus strong sales are one measure — you do begin to notice that those are works that tend to organize themselves around story (action), a cultural moment (time), place (location), or character (one unified subjectivity). You could do worse, at this stage in topic development, to think about those organizing rubrics. We see examples of them in many successful general audience books.

Falk, for example, tells his story through the eyes of one Benedictine monk in one cultural moment, not a half-dozen monks over a thousand years. One of my early general audience titles, *The Hotel on Place Vendôme,* was a book on the history of resistance at the Ritz Hotel in Paris (place) during the German occupation (time). Because that book took the perspective of multiple historical figures (no unity of character), unity of location in a delineated time period was the organizing principle. I included only events directly connected to the Ritz Hotel, even though it meant excluding some interesting adjacent archival discoveries. I started the book, as well, with a quotation that framed the book's unifying principle (and its main argument) for the reader: Joan Didion's observation in *The White Album,* "Great hotels have always been social ideas, flawless mirrors of the particular societies that they service." If you are struggling to decide if your topic has unity, looking for the one-sentence epigraph that would encapsulate its scope and purpose is also an effective tool for development.

For the moment, above all, keep in mind that academic books are not concerned with unity in the same way that general audience books are, and that for academics making the transition this will require some adjustment. Be prepared to edit. I often see book proposals from academics looking to make the transition to general audiences where there are multiple book ideas going on and where the proposed chapters are discontinuous. When working with an academic author on developing a nonfiction book proposal, I frequently will advise in these cases choosing one of those chapters and expanding it into a book idea. Not infrequently there is resistance. In fact, this is probably the most common critique that I offer of book proposals written by academic authors trying to place a general audience title: there will be too many things going on in one book proposal to unify the project.

General audience books also benefit from narrative and character. In order to write effective big trade nonfiction, you need to work with some kind of narrative. You need to have a narrative arc, in particular. This is something I get a lot of pushback on from academics looking to write a trade title. The argument against this, as it's been articulated to me inside the academy, is that it is possible to have a bestselling trade book that is simply expository. In other words, as an academic, one could write a book using the same organizational structures as in a monograph but reach a broad audience by speaking more plainly and in less specialized language. Perhaps there are exceptional cases in which that is true, but my experience is that this is not the rule.

Because I think narrative is central, I will discuss this in considerable detail later in this book, and you can come to your own conclusions then about whether you find what I have to say persuasive or not. For the moment, I want to say a bit about why I think this argument about the inclusion of narrative in general audience non-fiction matters and why I would urge academics to think about this topic in the developmental stages of a project.

I believe that the use of narrative and story matters. It matters not simply in terms of book sales — though that is surely going to be a factor, indeed the primary factor, for your editor and publisher. It matters for what it means for academics to be effective actors and agents in the public sphere. Academics being effective in the public sphere matters if we care about those same Enlightenment values that simultaneously opened the space for democracy and the university.

From the humanistic side of the cathedral and as a historian and theorist, here I could talk about the Enlightenment, the public sphere, and the republic of letters all being essentially narratological spaces. But let me make the argument instead from the neurological and scientific disciplines: there is also good peer-reviewed neuroscience showing that the incorporation of narrative storytelling (which includes the use of character) into our teaching and writing, even if we're not looking for a general audience book contract, helps the human brain process and communicate complex ideas. Enlightenment thinking is maybe three hundred years old. Our brains have been learning through storytelling for some thirty thousand years.

There is a growing body of work on this, and it is one of the reasons the sciences are, frankly, leading the way in communication for general audiences. In a recent multi-authored article published in October 2019 in the *Journal of Neuro-Science* (39:42, 8285–8290), titled "The Storytelling Brain," the researchers summarize the research and the stakes succinctly: "many scientists assume a standard lecturer approach when attempting to engage broad audiences, believing that, if the public is simply given more accessible information, societal support for scientific and technological issues will increase accordingly." This, however, is not what they found based on the evidence, which they described as follows:

> Narrative science storytelling may improve these efforts, helping to engage listeners and lead policy change. . . . In narrative storytelling, the narrator (or author) deliberately uses techniques, including voice, character, suspense, and description, to both connect the disparate elements involved and to create a compelling and readable story.

Reaching a broad audience is not just a matter of making complex information less specialized (although general audience authors need to do that, too). Narrative storytelling — the how and not just the what — matters for how people absorb and act on complex information as non-specialists. Narrative storytelling, in other words, combined with other strategies for reaching a broader audience and communicating effectively to non-specialists, just may be the difference between effective and ineffective public-facing expert communication.

If that is the argument for incorporating narrative into your general audience book, I have not heard any argument or seen any research, on the other hand, for why including narrative would be detrimental to a broad communication. Yes, it can be hard to learn to do, especially after years or even decades of writing in a different form. I don't see, however, that this in and of itself constitutes a good reason for excluding it as a communication strategy. For this reason, my unequivocal recommendation is that you look for topics where you can use narrative storytelling as a component of your project.

You can jump ahead to later chapters if you want to understand narrative more comprehensively at the generative stage. For the moment, as you are mulling ideas, my recommendation is to prefer subjects where there is a clear character or set of characters, or where there is a storyline, or both. Think of storyline for the time being as essentially about conflict (internal or external), a complication, and its resolution.

Finally, you need to know that your general audience project hasn't been done by someone else already as a general audience title and that, if you move forward with the topic, there is enough material to be able to write the book using fact-based communication. This does not mean you have to be the first person ever to write about your particular topic. If you are the first person ever to write about a topic, then you are probably working with a topic that is, in fact, too highly specialized to have broad market appeal. Writing a general audience title where there have been other academic monographs, however, isn't a deal breaker, although obviously you need to be doing your own research and not simply popularizing the research of other scholars.

If there has been a previous general audience title, things are a little more complex. Here, you want to be either the first person in the past decade or two and be able to offer something new, or to have a very clearly fresh take on the subject. The closer you are in time to a previous general audience book on the topic, the fresher that material or take needs to be. You should be aware, as well, that if there has been a previous general audience title on a subject, and if that previous title has not sold well, you will need to be able to make a strong argument for why that topic will be of broader interest now.

Resist the temptation to propose a general audience book unless you know where the new and relevant research material is located. Once you have a book contract in hand, there is a tendency for doors to begin to open, undeniably. I have often been able to arrange access to certain interviews, in particular, only once I could state that a book contract was in place. But you also want to be sure, before you accept the contract, that if you cannot secure access to particular material, you have sufficient access to other resources that will let you deliver on your project.

The general audience titles that we are discussing in this book are all fact-based projects, and as an academic it is particularly crucial that you honor what is known as the nonfiction contract. This is an agreement with your publisher, your editor, the media, and your readers that, while you are free to use all the devices of narrative storytelling — "voice, character, suspense, and description" — everything in your book will be based on research and source material. Even though you might not be able to incorporate all of the research behind a general audience title, the guarantee you are implicitly offering is that you could provide source citations for everything you say.

Chapter 2

THE TRADE MARKET AND THE "BIG" BOOK TOPIC

You have, then, some parameters to consider. What I've offered so far is a rubric to decide if an idea is big enough. What comes next is just plain old-fashioned brainstorming.

Although you can focus the generation of ideas on your particular area(s) of expertise, I'd also encourage you to think outside your field. If you know how to do fact-based research, expertise is whatever you choose to give sustained attention, and expertise is always evolving if we're intellectually curious.

Come up with a list of three or six or a dozen ideas and run them through the rubric for identifying a general audience topic that we outlined in the previous chapter. If an idea ticks all the boxes in the rubric or even all but one or two of the boxes, it's probably worth thinking about further. Often you will be able to check off those other missing boxes as you look at the idea more fully — or you will realize that, in fact, the idea didn't tick any of the boxes as well as you first anticipated.

Once you have a list of ideas that you want to consider, the next step is to see if someone else has already written this book as a trade title. The easiest way to find this information at the idea stage is to search Amazon.com. The site is a mega-aggregator, and in most cases it will pull up any title with similar keywords. You may need to try some different search terms to make sure you're pulling up books on the same topic and not just books with the same title you're imagining, but if you cast your net wide enough, it pretty reliably pulls up adjacent titles.

If you find another book has been published on your topic, don't discount the idea quite yet. Look at what that other book was specifically. If it's a trade title within the past decade or so, writing a new book on this topic is probably an uphill battle unless yours offers something that is very compellingly new and fresh, unless the topic is one of considerable and sustained general interest, or unless you have a particularly strong author platform, which is to say a culturally recognized voice on this topic. If it's a trade title from thirty years ago, on the other hand, it might be a good time for a new book on the topic. If the earlier title sold well and if that general interest in the topic now can be demonstrated, that's good. If the earlier title sold poorly and if there's no reason to believe the market of readers has grown? Not so good.

If what you're finding is an academic title, published on the academic list of a university press, that's not a deal breaker either. Academic titles and trade titles are simply apples and oranges. It's understood that academic titles, written as scholarly works, generally do not reach broad audiences or have more than extremely limited sales, and failing to sell ten thousand copies doesn't say anything, one way or the other, about whether there is general interest in the topic as a trade title. If there are other academic books on the topic, that's generally good news insofar as it suggests that there are historical or archival sources available, and their bibliographies are worth perusing carefully as well at later stages of topic development. But, beyond that, academic titles aren't comps and can be set aside.

So, too, can you set aside books that were self-published or were published at vanity presses, unless those titles happen to be recent bestsellers. These books also aren't comps because they didn't have the same distribution channels. If a self-published book sold very well and garnered considerable public attention, that would likely matter, but it might cut in either direction. A self-published book that sold well does suggest a strong market for a trade book on this topic. But then you have to weigh whether your title is bringing something new or better to the market. After all, it might be lower risk for the publisher just to reach out to the author of the self-published, proven title and try to acquire that book than to take a gamble on a book contract with an unproven author. But if the self-published book was written by an amateur author as a personal passion project and never reached the trade publishing sector, again: apples and oranges.

Topics that feature as a chapter in a broader title (*Ten Great Adventurers*, for example, when you want to write the biography of one of those great adventurers) are generally a positive sign for your book, especially if the broader title was trade and did well. That tends to suggest there is interest in this area, as well as scope to expand upon the topic, and that there is material. Novels based on your nonfiction book idea also aren't generally seen as competing titles and, if the novel does well or was published by a major imprint, can suggest an existing market demand that can be positive.

Be prepared for some frustration. In general, if you come up with ten good general audience ideas, you will find that in seven of those ten cases there has been a relatively recent trade book on the subject. There are hundreds of professional writers and their agents out there, looking every day for timely, fresh, relevant, narrative, gently contrarian, big book projects, and they and their editors tend to be tuned in to the publishing market. So be prepared to come up with a lot of ideas in the beginning, and be prepared to let those ideas go.

Once you have an idea that you think checks all the boxes and doesn't have directly competing titles that make a new book contract unlikely, you have to weigh that difficult question of bigness.

There are two essential components of a big trade-book idea. One of those things — the writing — you have a lot of control over. The other of those things — the market — you do not. Finding the story is a talent, and a great trade writer will want to develop it quickly. But there also have to be readers who are interested in the story.

So, before we look at how to find the story in your idea, as the first step to developing a book proposal and writing a bestselling trade title you need to take a long, hard look at your idea and see if there are really going to be ten thousand people or more interested enough in this topic to want to buy a copy of the book.

Why ten thousand copies? You could ballpark that number a bit lower, maybe five thousand copies if you're looking to place a title on the trade list of an academic press or an independent publisher. At one of the large publishing houses, the number is a lot more like thirty thousand copies or more. But ten thousand is a pretty good target number. Why? Put simply: it's the economic reality of trade publishing. It's important you understand how this market works if you want to enter it successfully. The logistics and the economics of book publishing shape the process of getting a general audience book accepted under contract in some fundamental ways, and the

———

more you understand about the market you are entering the better positioned you are to come up with an idea suited to becoming a trade title.

Let's start with academic publishing, which for most of us is the baseline. Academic titles are aimed at specialist audiences, and, because this is what hiring, tenure, and promotion committees reward, they are almost exclusively published by university presses operating on a non-profit basis or by a small number of trade publishers with strong academic lists, places like Taylor & Francis or Macmillan. Those trade publishers, I am reliably informed by editors, publish academic monographs as loss leaders. Academic titles are almost universally peer reviewed. Often trade titles on the lists of academic publishers are also peer reviewed (including this book). Like general audience books, academic books are, in fact, subject to the certain tests for timeliness and relevance; it's simply that those decisions are made substantially by anonymous peer reviewers rather than by editors or marketing teams.

For academic publications, the primary object is not sales. No one expects an academic monograph to make a profit for the publisher (though there are occasional pleasant surprises). Academic monographs have relatively small print runs, often only in the hundreds, and are generally aimed at the library market (so they are published in cloth or hard cover). The question academic publishers generally ask is how much a title is likely to cost the institution, not how much profit it is likely to generate, because it is not likely to generate any, either for the publisher or for the author. In "Reflections on University Press Publishing," published in *Academic Matters* in April 2009, Bill Harnum shared some startling Canadian academic press data showing that the average academic monograph loses for the press on average just a bit over ten thousand (Canadian) dollars, and I am also reliably informed that those figures, adjusted for some currency and inflation differences, are pretty consistent across the English-language academic market. Academic authors are paid in prestige. Academic presses are largely non-profit.

Broad audience titles are fundamentally trade titles: they are titles meant to be commercially successful. That means, as we've already said, one thing: sales of books. It means enough sales of books to offset the costs of production and make a profit for the company. There is a broad spectrum of publishers that publish trade titles. A number of academic presses, especially the larger and more prestigious university presses, have trade lists, where they publish broad-audience titles as a separate division. Most independent publishers, with the exception of certain art house non-profit presses, publish trade titles. And, of course, commercial publishers are publishing for trade and profit.

Among the commercial publishers, there is another spectrum. At the top of the hierarchy are the Big Five — the large multinational publishing groups that control an estimated 70–80 percent of the English-language book market. These are the publishing groups controlled by Penguin Random House, HarperCollins, Simon & Schuster, Hachette, and Macmillan. Among them, they own somewhere around five hundred different imprints. The rest of the book market is divided among a series of smaller independent publishers, such as (in the United States market) City Lights Publishers, New Directions Publishing, Verso Books, and Graywolf Press, among others.

This book is about how to transition from writing for academic audiences to writing for general audience readers, so by definition we are talking about how to publish trade titles, whether you choose to publish on the trade list of a university press, with a small independent publisher, or with one of the Big Five. The book proposal will look the same. Your process for testing and development of a general audience topic will look the same. You'll use the same chapter outlines. The royalties that you'll be offered in a contract will likely be indistinguishable. The scale and tempo, however, are likely to diverge, sometimes substantially. By that we mean that the scale of the projected sales, the intensity of the marketing, and the size of your advance will be variable. Big Five books are bigger, quite simply.

How exactly do we get to ten thousand copies as a ballpark figure? Consider your book, as a business proposition, from the perspective of the trade publisher. Book publishing is a business with relatively tight profit margins. Most trade publishers aim for a profit margin of fifteen percent and hope realistically to end up with at least a ten percent profit margin at the end of a fiscal year. Some of the open-access publishers are among the exceptions and enjoy fat profit margins of nearly forty percent on intellectual content that you provided to them for free or that perhaps you or your university paid a subvention to have them publish. For trade presses, however, the margins are between ten and fifteen percent in book publishing.

Where does the profit come from? Well, say a book retails for twenty dollars, a pretty average price for a trade paperback. The publisher is hoping to pocket not less than two dollars. Where does the rest of the sales price of a book go? Well, about half goes to wholesale discounts. Publishers need to make a profit, but so do bookstores. So publishers sell books to bookstores and other vendors at discounts that range from twenty-five to sixty percent off the retail price of the title. Forty to fifty percent is pretty common. Let's call it fifty percent on the back of the envelope. Twenty dollars, minus fifty percent, equals ten dollars. Out of these ten dollars, the publisher pays the cost of copy editing, typesetting, proofreading, printing, warehousing, shipping, and marketing a title. These are the direct costs. Direct costs per unit decrease as the number of copies printed increases. Publishers also have overhead: the salaries of their employees, the costs of running an office. These are relatively fixed costs unless a publisher is growing or contracting quickly. Publishers also absorb the costs of returns: the industry agreement under which bookstores and other vendors can purchase books for sale and then return to the publisher later, at the publisher's cost, any unsold product, to prevent discounting. Returns can run up to fifteen percent of a print run.

What you can see is that the only factors so far that are in a publisher's control are the direct costs — the costs of making and selling the actual book. Here, there are two levers. It costs the same amount of money to copy edit a thousand copies of a book as it costs to copy edit a hundred thousand copies. The larger the print run, the lower the unit cost per book. But that only works if those books are going to sell. One hundred thousand books might cost less per unit, but a hundred thousand unsold books still cost more than ten thousand unsold books. So a smart trade publisher is going to choose books positioned to reach a broad audience. As discussed earlier, it also costs more — and more than double — to print a book that is two hundred thousand words than to print a book that is a hundred thousand words. There is more paper, more shipping weight, more boxes, more copy editing.

Consumer expectations are that the suggested retail price — the price printed on the back cover — for a nonfiction paperback will range from seventeen to about twenty-five dollars, more or less irrespective of whether that paperback is fat or thin. Hardcover pricing on a title is generally ten dollars more than the paperback, typically running from twenty-seven to thirty-five dollars suggested retail for a hardcover. Publishers don't have a lot of flexibility in pricing. What they do have flexibility on are the terms of the contract and word limit. Publishers can also, within certain parameters, cut some production costs. They can outsource the printing. They can (and do) trim budgets on proofreading and fact-checking. This is why, as an academic, you always want to budget either time or money for your own additional fact-checking at the copy editing (or what is known as first pass) stage of production. If a book doesn't sell in the first few weeks after publication date, a publisher can trim the marketing budget and reallocate those resources to a more promising title.

And that's pretty much it. Because, out of the ten dollars left to a publisher after the discount, the trade publisher also has to pay one other thing: royalties. These are the payments to the author who produced the intellectual property, and royalties are pretty standard across the industry. Ten percent of the list price is extremely common on hardcover books. That typically moves up to twelve and a half or fifteen percent as the volume of sales increases. You might get paid twelve and a half percent, for example, after the sale of the first five thousand books. You will generally be paid seven and a half percent on paperbacks, moving up to ten percent with large volumes sold. You'll generally be paid twenty-five percent on e-books. Before you get too excited about e-books, keep in mind that twenty-five percent on e-books, which tend to be quite heavily discounted and which also tend to be paid "net" rather than "straight," usually ends up being less than your royalty on a paperback or hardcover. Royalties for physical books are generally paid on the retail price, but many of the large bookstore chains, for example, routinely discount the list retail price for new-release hardcovers by thirty percent. That comes out of an author's cut, as well as out of the publisher's and the seller's pockets.

I use the word "generally" as a repeated qualifier because we are talking here in generalities. There will be some variation in contracts, and variations are more likely if you have an agent negotiating these terms. Even with the world's hardest-nosed agent, however, there's not a huge amount of negotiating space on royalty percentages. These tend to be relatively standardized, in part because the margins in publishing are so tight. Where there can, however, be quite significant variation is in how and when these royalties are paid out: that is to say, advances.

Let's go back to that twenty-dollar retail paperback. Assuming it sells at twenty dollars (full suggested retail price) in the bookstore and assuming a fifty percent discount to the bookseller (from which all of his or her costs need to come to be profitable), you as the author are going to earn a dollar and fifty cents (seven and a half percent) of the remaining ten dollars. The publisher needs to return to owners and shareholders two dollars (ten percent). That means the publisher needs to cover all of the direct costs and overhead costs, including returns and remaindering unsold product, at six dollars and fifty cents per unit.

Royalties, however, are contracted in advance of sales. They also need to come out of the six dollars and fifty cents in the publisher's budget. For a trade book, a publisher is being asked to make a gamble. The publisher receives a book proposal for a book that has not yet been written. Based on that book proposal, the publisher has to make a calculated guess as to how many copies this book is going to sell, which entails making a guess about how many copies to print and what the unit price will be. This also involves making a guess to decide what the author will be guaranteed in respect to royalties.

———

A book advance is a guaranteed minimum of royalties the author is paid. It is literally an advance on royalties, and it is the amount that the author can count on earning, no matter how few copies of the book end up actually being sold, since the author doesn't pay back these advances if the book doesn't earn that much. Advances are typically paid out in three equal installments: on signing of the book contract, on delivery and acceptance ("D&A") of the publishable manuscript, and on publication (the day the book is released for sale, also called your "book birthday"). Sometimes you'll see a 50–25–25 percent split, or some other payout variations, but it would be highly irregular to receive the entire advance at the beginning or nothing until the end.

Just as an illustration (because the real numbers are more variable and complicated), let's assume you receive an advance of fifteen thousand dollars, and for each copy of your book sold you "earn" a dollar and fifty cents. That means that, for your advance of fifteen thousand dollars, the publisher is gambling that your book will sell ten thousand copies or more. If your book only sells a thousand copies, though, the advance is still yours. If your book sells the anticipated ten thousand copies — in the industry this is known as earning out — then you begin to receive royalties on every copy over that threshold, for as long as the book continues to sell. That can be decades. I continue to receive so-called residual royalties on my first trade book more than fifteen years later.

The trade editors I spoke with in fact-checking for this book agreed that for every thousand dollars of advance payment, six hundred and fifty books sold would be a good outcome for the publisher. The precise correlation between royalties and print runs can be variable, and is always case specific. You get the point, though: trade books are about sales.

How much, in general, are trade advances? Ten or fifteen thousand dollars is a nice advance on the trade list of a university press or with a small independent publisher, though I've personally heard of offers from trade lists at university presses reaching sixty thousand dollars. That's probably pretty exceptional, and fifteen thousand is a more typical nice number. Fifteen thousand dollars in advance is just a smidge under ten thousand copies.

Ten thousand readers, in other words, is an entry level number for a trade book. It is the smallest number of readers you should be imagining for your title when you're generating ideas, and books in this range are not typically *New York Times* bestsellers. These are good, solid, respectable trade sales at some of the more niche trade houses. The algorithms for the *New York Times* list are a subject of perennial intrigue and speculation in the industry, but there is a general sense among the editors and publishers I spoke with that hitting the list requires sales of about five thousand copies, from diverse vendors (so, no, you can't go order five thousand copies of your own book to buy bestseller status), per week. Per. Week.

If fifteen thousand dollars is a nice offer from an independent press or a university trade list, that same fifteen thousand dollar figure would be a very modest — and probably impossibly modest — advance from one of the Big Five publishers. Steve Laube, a literary agent with a good industry blog, in a post titled "What Are Average Book Sales?" (June 24, 2019), reports being told by one large publisher "that they have a threshold of 30,000 copies in projected sales" to consider a title. That means an advance of forty thousand dollars is a ground-floor number for a Big Five publisher. I asked three trade editors I know in New York City, and all confirmed that this is probably about where they would begin to consider a title, that advances from forty to sixty thousand are common for first-book offers, and that a nonfiction trade advance of a hundred thousand tends to be the "sweet spot." Those are books with projected sales of sixty-five thousand copies or more and, importantly, a hundred thousand dollars is still within the buying limits of most editors, making those books — if your idea is big enough — particularly attractive.

From another perspective, as of June 2022, the trade journal *Publisher's Weekly* reports in its "key" to book signings that a trade advance under fifty thousand dollars is a "nice deal," and one between fifty thousand and one hundred thousand is a "very nice deal," between one hundred and two hundred fifty thousand would be a "good deal," up to five hundred thousand a "significant deal," and an advance of five hundred thousand or more a "major deal." In my experience, for a first-time academic author writing trade nonfiction, an advance of somewhere between forty-five and eighty-five thousand would be a reasonable range of expectation — for a marketable, big enough, general audience idea with an excellent book proposal to a Big Five publisher.

The thing to keep in mind is that on any trade list, whichever publishing direction you end up taking, we are talking print runs and projected sales starting at somewhere between ten and thirty thousand copies, depending on where you position your title, for commercial publishers. Occasionally you might be able to place a book at one of the smaller houses with an anticipated print run of a few thousand copies and an advance in the range of five to ten thousand dollars for a particular topic. But in none of these cases are we talking about books with a worldwide audience of a few hundred potential readers. According to some industry data for 2020, published in "The Death of the Monograph" in *Publishing Research Quarterly* (38:382–395), the average academic monograph sells between two hundred and four hundred copies in the first three years of publication. In order to get a trade book contract, in the vast majority of cases your book proposal has to convince a publisher that this title can sell ten to thirty thousand copies or more—maybe much more—in two to three years (the timeline for a hardcover and then a paperback to release).

That is what it means for a trade book to be marketable. If you hear that your book idea isn't big enough, it means that the projected sales aren't enough to make the title attractive for a trade publisher. The game is not worth the candle.

So how do you know if your idea is big enough? Well, this is why in your book proposal you are going to be asked to give a market analysis. We will cover what this looks like and how to do a book proposal later, but it's worth giving it some thought while you're still weighing a list of ideas to develop.

Say you have an idea for a trade title. It ticks the boxes in our rubric. Your gut tells you there are going to be a lot of readers out there keenly interested in this book, but you want to check yourself before you set about the work of finding the story and writing a full book proposal, because frankly, writing a book proposal is a lot of work and can be a real pain in the butt.

What you need to do—because this is the first thing an agent or editor will do—is look at comparative titles. Make a list of six to twelve books, published in the last few years, and certainly not more than a decade ago at the outside, that are reasonably comparable to the book you are imagining. The operative term is "reasonably." Prince Harry's *Spare* is not a good comp for your biography of King George III, in spite of the family connection. Prince Harry's tell-all is a comp for books in the major celebrity memoir category, and the comps for your biography of King George III are historical biographies of royals and public figures. "Recent" is also an operative term. Published in the past couple of years is ideal, because the market is variable.

Once you have a broad range of comps, go look up the sales figures. To do this, get yourself a subscription to access the trade site *Publisher's Marketplace* (www.publishersmarketplace.com). You will need to purchase access, which you can do either monthly (no long-term commitment) or on a day-access pass, and unfortunately it's not inexpensive. Personally, I think paying for the subscription cost is a reasonable thing to ask a dean to cover, if your institution is at all serious about supporting academics looking to write for broader audiences. A subscription includes a sales database known as "BookScan," and this is what everyone in the industry uses for reference. On *Publisher's Marketplace* you can research book sales, book trends, and agents.

If those comps are coming back with sales of more than ten thousand copies, that's good news. If those comps are coming back with sales over thirty thousand copies, great news. If the comps are coming back with sales lower than ten thousand copies, it's time to have a think. Possibly you didn't choose good comparative titles, and you need to look for other recent book publications that might better showcase your project. I'd certainly start there. But it's also possible that your idea is not as big as you'd hoped. In that case, it's better to know that now, before you put a lot of work into developing a book proposal that isn't likely to get a contract.

Chapter 3

FINDING THE STORY

You have a marketable idea with strong comps. What next? Section one of a book proposal is a narrative summary: a succinct pitch in which you showcase your trade idea and show that you can write a trade title.

We're going to spend the final chapters of this book looking at how writing for trade and general audiences works at a sentence level. You can jump ahead to those sections if you wish. For the moment, we're going to focus on finding the story or the narrative arc in your general audience idea so you can write the narrative summary (and can practice finding the story, something you'll need to do repeatedly once you have that contract and are writing). Nonfiction is fact-based writing, so you are going to need some material. Then, you are going to have to look at that material with the critical eye of a trade author. Somewhere in the facts that constitute your topic, there is a narrative arc. In fact, there are many possible narrative arcs. The job of the writer is to find one.

So what is narrative? Here are a couple of propositions that we're going to be working with and expanding upon throughout this book: the first is that narrative moves from conflict through complication to resolution. You need to find in your material all three of those entanglements. Second, there are three main elements of narrative nonfiction: story (narrative), character, and meaning (idea). You want to find all three. Third, there are three basic narrative patterns: linear (plot or narrative driven, featuring conflict, crisis, and resolution), circular (character driven, meaning the character changes from the beginning to the end of the story), or enveloping narratives (one story within another story). You will also need to decide which of these works best as a vehicle. You can mix patterns. And, finally, while plot moves from conflict to resolution, narrative also works with periodic tightening and loosening of the tension threads of story. This is narrative tension. You will need to learn how to loosen and tighten the threads of your narrative. Character is generally involved.

What does this look like in practice? We'll look at two examples. But first steps first. Once you have a strong general audience topic, your next step should be to summarize the book idea in three hundred to seven hundred words; your ideal target would be five hundred words. Imagine you are writing the description on the front flap of your book's jacket. The best way to research this next step is to take a stroll in a good, large bookstore, in the section or sections most relevant to the category of general audience book that you're considering. Look at some front flaps. Read the marketing material on the back of the jacket or (especially for hardcovers) on the inside dustcover flaps. What you're looking to learn here is the diversity of ways in which general audience authors in your area communicate their relevance and broad market appeal to readers.

By way of a first example, until you can browse that bookshop, here is the actual front flap material for one of my recent general audience books. I cannot claim authorship of this material: it is written in-house (and, therefore, is reflective of what the publisher sees as broad market about this title).

In a tale as twisted as any spy thriller, discover how three women delivered critical evidence of Axis war crimes to Allied forces during World War II: "Mazzeo is a fascinating storyteller" (*New York Journal of Books*).

In 1944, news of secret diaries kept by Italy's Foreign Minister, Galeazzo Ciano, had permeated public consciousness. What wasn't reported, however, was how three women — a Fascist's daughter, a German spy, and an American socialite — risked their lives to ensure the diaries would reach the Allies, who would later use them as evidence against the Nazis at Nuremberg.

In 1944, Benito Mussolini's daughter, Edda, gave Hitler and her father an ultimatum: release her husband, Galeazzo Ciano, from prison, or risk her leaking her husband's journals to the press. To avoid the peril of exposing Nazi lies, Hitler and Mussolini hunted for the diaries for months, determined to destroy them.

Hilde Beetz, a German spy, was deployed to seduce Ciano to learn the diaries' location and take them from Edda. As the seducer became the seduced, Hilde converted as a double agent, joining forces with Edda to save Ciano from execution. When this failed, Edda fled to Switzerland with Hilde's daring assistance to keep Ciano's final wish: to see the diaries published for use by the Allies. When American spymaster Allen Dulles learned of Edda's escape, he sent in socialite Frances De Chollet, an "accidental" spy, telling her to find Edda, gain her trust, and, crucially, hand the diaries over to the Americans. Together, they succeeded in preserving one of the most important documents of WWII.

Drawing from in-depth research and first-person interviews with people who witnessed these events, Mazzeo gives readers a riveting look into this little-known moment in history and shows how, without Edda, Hilde, and Frances's involvement, certain convictions at Nuremberg would never have been possible.

The idea here is to give a concise and economical (this comes in at just over three hundred words) summary of what makes this book compelling to a general audience and to tick those development boxes for an editor or reader.

Here is another example of a book summary. This one I did write and used in a successful grant application to the National Endowment for the Humanities Public Scholar program, for a trade-book idea that I was developing during the period when I was drafting this book for publication.

Mary Ann Patten was nineteen when her husband's extreme clipper ship, *Neptune's Car*, set off from New York City in the summer of 1856 with heavy mining equipment destined for San Francisco and the California Gold Rush in the hull. *Neptune's Car* had already broken the speed record for travel between New York and Calcutta, and now they were part of an extreme clipper race of four competing vessels, attempting to make the journey around the tip of South America, from New York to California, in fewer than one hundred days. What occurred on that race is a quite astonishing story, replete with a mutinous first mate hired by another captain to disable *Neptune's Car* (and prepared to shipwreck them) and the collapse of Mary Ann's young husband, Captain Joshua Patten, just as they were coming into the dangerous Straits of Lemaire at the entrance to the Cape Horn archipelago, the result of meningitis brought on by the "white plague," the global tuberculosis epidemic that would peak, at last, that decade in the United States. Mary Ann takes the helm, fends off the attempted mutiny, gains the acclamation of the crew, steers the 216-foot clipper though an eighteen-day gale off Antarctica and sixty-foot waves using the maritime books in the ship's library (and her very good sense), navigates by the stars through icebergs when they are blown off course by the storm near Antarctica, and, ultimately, arrives in San Francisco, at the helm and heavily pregnant, having managed to keep her husband alive, with $350,000 worth of cargo intact, in second place in the race.

The international press in 1856, unsurprisingly, went wild for this story of epic maritime adventure, covering every detail in breathless reporting. Mary Ann Patten was a celebrity from San Francisco to London. The $1,000 in prize money she was awarded by the insurers, in thanks for having saved the ship and the cargo, caused public outrage at being far too paltry a sum to recognize the feat of the "Florence Nightingale of the Seas" (as *The New York Times* dubbed her), especially when readers learned that the ship's owners refused to pay Captain Patten's $3,000 in wages due to his infirmity on the voyage, leading to more scandalized press coverage and a fund raiser for additional prize money.

A few decades later, the suffragettes, advocating for the civil rights of women as United States' citizens, adopted Mary Ann Patten as an icon and example of women's equal capacities, renewing her acclaim, and in the 1930s the United States' Merchant Marine Academy recognized Mary Ann Patten's accomplishments as a mariner with few equals, male or female, and marked her untimely death by naming the campus hospital after her. Because, sadly, Mary Ann Patten did not live to make another voyage. She also died at age twenty-four, from the "white plague" she contracted while nursing her husband on board their Antarctic voyage.

This new biography of Mary Ann Patten, drawing on fresh research into unpublished women's maritime journals, local archives, and the contemporary press, brings her story and the story of the extreme clipper races that built nineteenth-century global America to life for readers of history and adventure.

—

This narrative summary comes in at five hundred and thirty words, right around my target length of about five hundred words, and, if you read through the text, you should be able to identity the places where I am ticking those boxes.

Let's go through the developmental checklist I've suggested you can use to double-check yourself:

1. Does this topic have character potential? (Yes, Mary Ann Patten is a character.)

2. Does this topic have narrative potential? (Yes, there are lots of options here, ranging from maritime adventure to the mutiny, the storm at sea, the clipper race, all containing elements of conflict.)

3. Can I see how to keep the focus of the book tight and unified? (Yes, the easiest way to focus the book would be to keep to the chronological period of the clipper ship race, from departure to arrival, using Mary Ann Patten's character as a secondary unifying device within that frame.)

4. Is it gently contrarian? (Yes, it's the untold story of a forgotten heroine.)

5. Can I see how to move the idea from narrow to broad to reach a wide audience? (Yes, Mary Ann Patten's specific story tells us something broader about clipper ship races, Antarctica, the California Gold Rush, the founding of the United States and women's role in it, globalization and pandemics.)

6. Are there any cultural trends supporting or (more importantly) undercutting this book in the next year or two? (Yes, there are cultural trends, such as "Me Too," supporting a market for books on strong women in history; there is the contemporary relevance of Antarctica and the climate crisis; there are not any obvious cultural trends undercutting the topic.)

7. Can I imagine a broad range of readers and explain how the topic is timely to a publisher? (Yes, sure, this is a story about a particular woman who did something courageous and interesting, but it is also a great adventure story in general, about Antarctica, a part of the world that is in the news due to climate change. This is also a story about the tuberculosis pandemic, and pandemics are newsworthy and will likely continue to be for the next few years.)

8. Do I know where to find the material? (Yes, there is good archival material in places I can identify and where access is unrestricted.)

9. Has someone else already written the book that I am imagining? (No.)

10. Have I outlined a narrative in my summary that has conflict, complication, and resolution as an arc? (Yes, there is a race, complicated by a storm and a mutiny, and a resolution, e.g., survives storm, puts down mutiny, comes in second place.)

11. Have I told a story in which there is a narrative (above), moved forward by characters, in order to offer meaning? (Sure, there are lots of characters, and lots of characters in conflict with different motives, and conclusions this story draws about the Gold Rush, clipper races, American history, women's resilience, and so on.)

12. Is there a narrative structure in place? (Yes, this is a linear narrative primarily, and it works with some enveloping structure in order to focus the biography of Mary Ann Patten on a relatively narrow part of her life. After all, I'm not really interested in her early childhood.)

13. Is there loosening and tightening of narrative tension? (Yes, Mary Ann Patten steers the ship through the storm—only to be tricked again by the first mate and again imperiled. They run out of the storm—but right into new danger in Antarctica.)

Will this book go on to become a *New York Times* bestseller? Maybe. But a lot of things go into making a *New York Times* bestseller besides a strong general audience topic. Some of those things have to do with skill and writing, and some have to do with luck, timing, and factors for which we can't control.

So far, though, this is a pretty solid narrative summary. It was successful in its purpose. It's succinct and has the core of a narrative arc. I can slot this into my book proposal. Down the road, I can pull a few of those sentences in the first paragraph out and use them to shape a one- or two-sentence pitch in my cover letter.

Note that what I've done so far is just enough research to have a command of the material available, without having actually started any writing. In my view, it is crucial not to lock yourself in with any actual writing until you've laid out a narrative arc. Once you have your narrative summary, you're ready to move on to the next chapter.

Chapter 4

FROM NARRATION TO NARRATIVE

Writing this book, I struggled for a long time with how to explain, in concrete and useful terms, the difference between academic writing and writing for general audiences. There are so many variables, and so much of what I have learned came through trial and error and the unspoken work of daily practice. Truthfully, it was not until writing my fourth trade book that I realized I had reached a certain level of fluid mastery where things started to feel intuitive. There is so much that I could say, but saying it requires a litany of caveats, the most important of which is that good storytelling is relentlessly specific. But let's try to sketch out some broad principles you can use in writing your first trade title.

This chapter focuses on the structural issues that distinguish academic expository writing from trade writing and is intended to help you think through how to structure the chapter summaries in your book proposal — and ultimately the chapters in your project. Chapter summaries are the second section of a book proposal, at least as I order proposals. Later chapters of this book focus on the paragraph- and sentence-level tools that you can use to move your writing in the direction of what we have been talking about through-out this book as effective narrative.

Early in my own writing for general audiences, what I heard time and time again was that my writing was still too academic. I think, more than fifteen years later, I understand what is meant by this, and it is closely related to the topic of thesis and argument. So let's circle back now and return to the question of how thesis in general audience writing is different from the expository structure of academic prose in concrete terms.

Think again about what we are trying to accomplish in academic prose. The over-arching goal, repeated as a mantra in promotion and tenure committees, is "making an original contribution to knowledge." That typically means that we are either presenting new research or making a new argument, or both. That new research might be a scientific study or newly recovered archival material. It might be a fresh archaeological discovery, a new fragment of DNA, or a new fragment of poetry. Something, however, needs to be new, because the goal is for our contribution to knowledge to be "original."

As academics, we not only need to present this original contribution, but we also need to follow certain disciplinary procedures to prove that our contribution is both valid and original. In academic prose, the author-scholar is always being evaluated by peers and judged for whether we have successfully presented our evidence and made our argument. Much of the work of academic prose is analytic: we present our claims, we present our evidence, and we show how our evidence is proof of the claims we are making. There are certain cultural differences, of course. In the North American system, the argument tends to be deductive. In the British system, for the humanities at least, the argument tends to be inductive. But, even as the order in which the operations are performed can vary, the project is essentially expository.

Academic writing, it seems to me, creates an odd double feint. On one hand, the disciplinary conventions are that the facts drive the argument. Academic prose, even when it uses the first person, which is by no means the norm in many academic disciplines, tends to sublimate authorial voice. Conventionally, the voice is author evacuated. The writing can be energetic and active. Some academic writers are fine stylists. But the thesis and the evidence are meant to take center stage, and an academic author should not upstage his or her own argument.

On the other hand, if anything, the problem with academic writing, from the perspective of a general audience reader and a trade editor, is that the author stance is too intrusive. Even as we conventionally efface the personality of the writer in academic prose, it is always about us, showing to our peer readers that we have met the bar of proof for how we know what we say we know, performing the disciplinary rituals of showing we have made an original contribution. In the academy, after all, the very notion of a thesis — the most fundamental of which is the dissertation — is that it is a work intended to have to be defended by its author, *viva voce*. We all go through the ritual of the public defense precisely so that we understand we are never not personally responsible for our research and our arguments. In our writing, we replicate this institutional practice, mostly as a trained habit. The result is that, however cloaked his or her individual personality may be, the implied academic author — the author stance — is always present, always attesting to the integrity and originality of the work, always working to make the argument (and to undermine or qualify any counter-argument) for a skeptical expert reader. Put mostly bluntly, as academics we tend to be *narrators* rather than to write *narrative*.

—

Here, if we make another checklist, are what I see as some of the typical features of academic writing. Academic writing tends to do the following.

1. Take an expository approach, in which the logical connections among thesis, evidence, and conclusion are explicitly stated. There is a narratorial mind building those connections, which is to say constructing argument. This tends to necessitate a relatively linear and deductive progression, in which thesis, evidence, analysis, and conclusion proceed in a stable order.

2. Place the author (in a narrative stance) between the reader and the content. The author-researcher is understood to be making the argument and to be responsible for doing so effectively (and to a professional presumed audience). He or she is the mediator of knowledge: the professor. This is true whether the academic author uses a first-person voice, third-person voice, or passive constructions.

3. Prioritize making a new contribution to knowledge, often including explicit framing of the scope of that knowledge or field of contribution.

4. Establish authority through the use of discipline-specific terms or paradigms and through (often passing) reference to foundational prior research. In the humanities especially, this tends also to include the specialist language of theory and references to theoretical constructions that are assumed to be shared by disciplinary readers and presumed to exclude non-specialists. There is a focus on establishing oneself as part of a larger (implied) conversation, which is not the primary subject of exposition but is a primary basis of authorial authority.

5. Be generically self-referential. There tend especially to be generic references to the prestige genres of the academy: argument, article, and monograph. Expressions such as "I will argue in this chapter" or "This book focuses on" are not uncommon.

——

Habituated academic readers tend not to notice them because they function, much like the indentation at the start of a new paragraph, primarily as conventional organizational markers.

6. Emphasize the testing of knowledge and argument, often against an explicitly stated counter-argument. There is often an expectation that the academic author will include facts contrary to his or her argument and will proceed to explain why those counter-facts can be dismissed or bracketed.

7. Focus on content as a generalized object, rather than as a specific subjectivity. Academic writing would tend, for example, to talk about "the jellyfish" seen from the perspective of the observer, rather than to talk about "a jellyfish" and its perspective. Academic writing has subjects and not characters.

How is this different from general audience writing? General audience arguments, perhaps most importantly, are not primarily expository, even — and perhaps especially — when they are big-idea focused. It is not that general audience books don't make arguments, point to meaning, or have a thesis. However, the way in which that thesis is developed is fundamentally different.

One way to think about the thesis in a general audience book is that it proceeds through leitmotif rather than exposition. *Leitmotif* is a term with an interesting history, perhaps especially because it was popularized after World War I by the German novelist Thomas Mann, as a way of thinking about the narration of history and its relationship to the constitution of the public sphere in the shadow of the Weimar Republic. The origins of the term, however, are primarily musical. A leitmotif is a tonal repetition. The German root meaning is something like "a leading motive" or perhaps even "a motivated leading."

General audience argument offers readers the subtle repetition and deepening of a thesis through illustration (and often through

story) and leaves the reader to draw the connection among the ac-
cumulating instances of repetition and variation. It is a "motivated"
repetition that builds to a conclusion. Think of leitmotif as the "evidence" in an academic argument. Writing for a general audience is
different from academic prose in that the author is not performing
for the reader the disciplinary procedure of linking or elucidating
how the evidence illustrates the claim. The writer presents the thesis
(or theme), offers the evidence from various angles and in various
tonalities, as discrete story occasions, and trusts the reader to articulate for him or herself the synthesis and conclusion. The role of
the reader is larger, the role of the author as explainer is smaller, and
the structure is not necessarily linear. It is certainly not deductive.
There can be, for example, circular or frame narrative (enveloping)
structures when argument proceeds by leitmotif.

The early American writer Nathaniel Hawthorne, who had a
knack for choosing resonant and dynamic examples in his national
tales, talked about the importance of identifying facts that have a
certain luminosity: facts that emit cultural energy. In his piece "The
Maypole of the Merry-Mount" (1836), Hawthorne spoke of seek-
ing out "facts [that have] wrought themselves almost spontaneously
into a sort of allegory." General audience writing does not need to be
overtly allegorical ("other" or double speaking, in effect), and it does
not need to be a national tale. However, where an argument proceeds by leitmotif, choosing repetitions that carry within them the
kernel of their own story and meaning is also central for developing
what, in trade publishing, your agents and editors will speak of as
narrative arc.

What we're talking about then are alternate modes of argumentation in general audience writing. In conventional academic writing, the author's presence is thick. The author is making the

argument and persuading the reader, even when the author is apparently invisible. In writing for general audiences, the narrative arc carries that weight. In general, if I had one sound-bite piece of advice for academically trained authors wanting to write trade narrative nonfiction and struggling with the arc, it's this: get out of the way. Less narration. More narrative.

This does not mean that there is no authorial voice or presence in a general audience book. Quite the contrary. A writer in a trade book can absolutely appear as a character. But the author's appearance is *as* character, like any other character. The author becomes part of a general audience book, on occasion, but the author does not put him or herself between the reader and the story. The writer offers the story and then lets the story go. That means the power and the skill of the trade author rely, fundamentally, on selection.

Let me use one last conceptual example, which has nothing to do with narratology, to try to imagine the difference between academic and trade writing. Think about the sport of technical rock climbing. I once had a boyfriend who was an elite technical rock climber, and I spent a lot of time in my younger life sitting at the bottom of a cliff, bored, thinking. There are two ways of rock climbing at the elite level: climbing with protection and free soloing. When you go rock climbing with protection, you are climbing with safety ropes and following an established course studded with bolts. As you ascend the cliff, you pause along the route at each bolt to attach your safety rope to the rock face with a carabiner.

Academic writing involves developing a thesis with protection. The disciplinary conventions act as bolts, securing our shared path toward argument and original knowledge. It is important not only to clip into the bolts of exposition and analysis as waypoints, but it is important to be *seen* to be clipping into those bolts. It is important, in other words, for the author-researcher to be seen as showing in academic prose why and how you know what you say you know. That includes everything from footnotes or endnotes to specific disciplinary terms to genre conventions in the academy.

Writing for general audiences, on the other hand, is free soloing that same route. The fundamental difference is, simply, that you do not clip into the bolts on your route to proving a thesis. As a nonfiction author, you need to use all the same safeguards. You have to develop the idea as well as the story. You cannot invent material, even if there are no footnotes for readers. You pass the same bolts in your ascent. You will be held to account for reaching the same end point. Your colleagues and deans will make sure of it, never mind the online comments of your public readers, who will be among the toughest critics you will ever have. But in a trade book, one doesn't write "In this chapter I will argue," because one of the most persistent bolts of academic prose is just this reference back to the route one is following.

The fact is, for general audience readers, the expository performativity of writing that is too academic is just boring. No one wants to watch you clipping into your bolts. No one outside the professional club enjoys reading prose that makes insider references. About critical theory, in particular, let me say this, one insider to another, as someone who earned a joint Ph.D. from the University of Washington program in theory and criticism circa 1999 and who still considers theory supremely interesting: general readers do not just find the language of theory annoying. They find it absolutely infuriating. It is not just a couple of bolts. It's a cliff face covered with guano and tagged with graffiti.

In trade writing, the reader performs a far more active narratological role, and he or she will either clip the bolts along the way, or not. Some readers will put together the idea and find in the book you write the meaning, or a meaning. Other readers will simply be carried along by character and story. Others will decide the book is tedious and will just stop reading. A poll taken in 2015 by the *National Post* in Canada and published in an article by the journalist Sadaf Ahsan had a sobering headline: "Only sixty per cent of books purchased are ever opened" (September 16, 2015). Making a reader make the argument is not your responsibility — or in your power. All you can really do is write a book that a reader wants to read, one that reader might open and perhaps continue reading, and make judicious selections in good faith. And tell one hell of a story.

I want to say a little bit more about that question of good faith and also about how academic discourses of originality can make the process of transitioning to writing for general audiences more difficult. When I am talking with academics working on a trade-book proposal, they are often anxious about sharing their idea for a topic. On several occasions, I've been asked to sign a non-disclosure agreement before reading a draft. I have no particular objection to signing a piece of paper if it makes a prospective author feel reassured, but my heart sinks every time, because what I immediately suspect is that this person is laboring under a set of mistaken assumptions that we are going to have to sort out long before we can productively talk about an actual book proposal.

I understand where the worry comes from. In the academy, we are judged on our ability to produce, at a sustained pace over a period of decades, original contributions to knowledge. We work in relatively narrow fields. There are economic and prestige consequences. Resources and permanent, tenurable positions are limited. All of this contributes to a culture of scarcity and a terror that someone might try to scoop our research. We add to this the unknown terrain of the trade world, where we're told that the economic stakes are even higher, and it's easy for even the most rational person to get a little paranoid.

This is not a nightmare that keeps trade authors up at night. That is because what trade authors know is that we live in a sea of facts. If, in the world of trade writing, your original contribution to knowledge is reformulated, so that what makes it original and a contribution is the judicious selection of material, rather than discovery, there is no way for any one writer ever truly to scoop another. The facts that you select will always be different from the facts that I select — though we probably both should be looking for those luminous facts that have the power of "spontaneous allegory" for our particular projects. Even if our facts were the same, along the path of writing there are so many crossroads and directions that we would not arrive in the same way at the same destination regardless. Certainly, if one of us published a trade book first, and what was timely or relevant about this topic now were exhausted, that might make placing a second trade book harder, but when book deals are routinely announced in *Publisher's Marketplace* and with lead times in the years for publication, this isn't a likely scenario. If someone got to your trade idea first and you know about it, she got to that idea months, probably years, ahead of you.

I have seen precisely this collision of academic and trade-writing worlds collide on social media, for instance in May 2022, when the *New York Times* published a series of articles on reparations in Haiti. One article was a nonfiction piece on the history of this issue, positioned, unsurprisingly, as timely, relevant, and something not broadly known to the general reader. Another article was a "Look Under the Hood" piece, outlining some of the sources behind that article, for interested readers. The author of the first piece was a correspondent with twenty years of journalism experience and the author of trade nonfiction.

One of the sources for the article was a senior Harvard professor, whom the journalist interviewed on background—meaning the source was not the topic of the piece, was not featured in the piece, and was not quoted—and who took umbrage online at not having her work publicly credited. Very quickly, a good number of social media followers made supportive comments, tagging the *New York Times* and the journalist. Those who were academics almost universally agreed that the use of the professor's thoughts was unethical. Other followers, who worked in trade journalism, pointed out that it would in fact be rare for a journalist to credit sources who were interviewed only on background.

I'm not commenting on who is right or wrong, and that is precisely because I can see so clearly what has happened. This is a classic example of how academics get the trade writing world wrong—and how trade writers, for their part, unwittingly blow past the "bolts" that matter to the academy and for academic reputation. The Harvard professor argued, implicitly and correctly within the academy, that what is original about her work is the archival labor guaranteed by certain facts in her knowledge possession. She deserves, by the standards of the academy, to enjoy the prestige of acknowledgment as the mediator of this knowledge. The senior journalist, on the other hand—and correctly within the world of trade publishing—sees that what is original about her work is the judicious selection of material and the way she crafts the story. She interviewed a Harvard professor on background. The Harvard professor did not invent and does not own the facts. Unless the Harvard professor was quoted, citation would not be expected in the world of the journalist. Background sources are not the story. That is not the same framework as in the academy.

It is an online controversy that, in the accelerated news cycle of social media, will undoubtedly be long forgotten by the time this book appears in print — by everyone except the principals. The collision, however, matters, I think.

For one thing, it matters if you are an academic looking to transition into the world of writing for general audiences. It matters especially if you are an academic looking to straddle these two different knowledge systems. There is a pragmatic and reputational reason for understanding the different rules of each of these systems, but I think there is also a larger and more philosophical reason why academics holding on perhaps a little less tightly to the ownership and regulation of knowledge matters.

Perhaps it is a sign that I have lived too long in the world of trade writing. I suspect, rather, that it was my early academic interest in history from the bottom that led me to writing for general audiences, and that this has worked in my career in the other direction. Whatever the genealogy, I do believe, as a fundamental tenet, that from the same set of facts, we can tell innumerable stories, make dozens of arguments. I believe this matters deeply for the work of the public sphere and for liberal democracy. This is precisely why, for the center to hold, the ways facts have been undermined in a post-truth era are so pernicious. The public sphere, when it functions to hold open the space of democracy, is the visible place in which rational actors come to tell their different and multiple stories, based on a shared set of first principles.

This is why an academic author setting out to tell deliberately provocative and sophistical public-facing stories would be such a gross violation of good faith. When intelligent citizens turn their minds to taking a set of facts and spinning from them vile absurdities that mock the public sphere, they have become Tucker Carlson.

The corollary, however, is also this: when academics enter the public sphere, that contested realm of story, to communicate fact-based arguments with cultural relevance and significance, that is work worth doing. When that work is communicated in ways that have the power to allow citizens to change their own minds and, thereby, to shape policy and politics, that is being a public intellectual. When we enter the public sphere, though, the facts are the story; we, author-researchers, are not. That is different from what happens in the academic arena where the author-researcher acts as maestro and mediator. When we enter the public sphere, "our" facts do not belong to us any longer either. That is what makes them public.

What, then, does developing a general audience thesis look like in practice? We proceed by leitmotif. We are looking for facts that shape themselves into "spontaneous allegory," and we are looking, in a replication of the public sphere itself, to create the space of idea, meaning, and story in which informed citizens are encouraged and empowered to draw conclusions and make judgments without having to take the word of the expert.

All of my trade books have had a thesis and made an argument, of a sort, and I use the leitmotif and spontaneous allegory principles actively. One strategy I've found effective is using an epigraph to introduce the leading theme, as I've mentioned. My thesis in *The Hotel on Place Vendôme* was that, to understand the complexity of experience during the German occupation, a domestic space that was also internationally iconic, such as the Ritz Hotel, in which different classes and categories of people lived in close proximity, offered an important archival and historical subject. Nowhere, however, do you find that sentence or anything like it in the book. Instead, I let that quotation from Joan Didion about great hotels being flawless mirrors of the society they service, placed on the first page, do the work of introducing the thesis.

The remainder of the book, which was working overtly with a series of national tales, is structured as variations and intensifications of the idea. One chapter tells the story of a Jewish bartender, who aids a small but brave German resistance, standing in front of the vast mirrored Ritz bar. Another chapter is the tale of a drug-addled Hermann Göring dressed in flamboyant semi-drag, attempting to hide from Hitler—a reflection of so many who tried not to look beyond the corridors of luxury. The last chapter tells of the hotel's French managing director and his American-born Jewish wife, who survived her time in a Gestapo prison only in body, and their murder-suicide which takes place with an old service revolver, decades after the war, on the day of his forced retirement. It is a national tale many lived for years after the war ended. These histories are spontaneous allegories that make their own arguments.

On other occasions, I've taken different approaches. In a historical book about the heroism and atrocities of the Warsaw Ghetto (*Irena's Children*), my thesis was an admittedly angry one. I know more about how the Gestapo killed people than anyone probably should, and, like most scholars of genocide, I have had moments of fury at our cultural forgetting and especially our nonchalance about our responsibility for the children of others. My big idea in that book was to write a history so granular and simultaneously so void of melodrama, inhabited by characters who were seen whole and complete, with all their flaws and with all their bravery, that the reader felt compelled to ask, "What would I do in the face of fascism?" I did

—

a huge amount of research into the sights, sounds, and smells of occupied Warsaw. What I wanted was for readers to sit with me in narrative time and to imagine the unimaginable.

Accomplishing that meant, ironically, not recounting the horrors as I knew them as a scholar. You cannot beat a reader over the head with what you know as an expert. Realistically, a reader will tolerate only one or two moments of intense discomfort in a book before deciding that the book is too hard or too painful (or, worse, too boring) to read and set it aside. So helping a reader to sit and imagine what I have *not* written and could not likely persuade him to read, but which he can piece together from the facts presented to him, meant drawing the reader into a world so granular that it felt real, followed by one or two moments of raw historical narrative, and then making it clear to a reader that you are holding back out of compassion. I'll talk more about using silence and "writing the gap" as a narrative tool in the chapters on writing at the level of the sentence.

I am not arguing that the ways in which I have tried to approach certain writing problems are (or are not) the precise techniques that you want to adopt or that will fit your project. My point, rather, is that general audience theses do not function in the same way as academic theses. If you want to avoid champagne lunches with your editor and to avoid hearing those words, "too academic," try to reformulate how you think about thesis, how much responsibility you pass to a reader, and alternate modes of argumentation. And remember that, when you are writing propulsive narrative, in which the reader is given the freedom to string together the thread of pearls that constitute story, it requires thinking strategically about the thread, the pearls, and the space between them.

You can have a big idea in your trade book. You can call that big idea a thesis if you wish. The key thing to double-check yourself on is simply that you have structured your idea in a way that it remains an effective general audience topic. As I have said, however, it's my firm belief that, in order to do this effectively, you ultimately need narrative, and particularly, a narrative arc that spans the space of the title.

There are entire other books that could be written about (and have been written about) narrative and storytelling, and this section is not in any sense exhaustive. But if you are coming to this topic for the first time and are looking for a point of entry, the two central narrative devices are story and character. These are, strictly speaking, two distinct facets. I'm going to talk about them in tandem because they tend to be mutually reinforcing and, when things are working well, intricately connected.

What is story? Or, perhaps more bluntly, what makes a good story? Think of the central metaphor we use for story: a story is a thread. We "spin a good yarn." We have "tangled tales." At the end, we have a denouement, an untangling. In a story, one thing follows from another thing, in an unbroken thread (a unity), something tangles, then comes straight.

At its simplest, narrative is the form of story in which the thread moves from conflict through complication to resolution. Rising action, climax, and falling action are the simplest units of story, but rarely is an effective narrative that threadbare. Effective storytelling tends to be multi-nodal, or, if we want to carry on with the thread metaphor, more complexly woven, more complexly strung. The conflict and tension, in other words, typically tighten and loosen more than once before a final resolution. This tightening and loosening, this slippage from one node to the next, are what we mean when we talk about narrative pacing.

———

For any book, you want to think about some form of pacing, even if your project is primarily a big idea book rather than overtly narrative focused. We had said earlier that there were — speaking in the broadest of generalities — three types of structure: those carried by the propulsion of narrative; those functioning through expansion and contraction of a big idea like an accordion to create the movement of story; and those using unity of character to organize and map a history. All three structures work, as we have already seen, with narrative or an aspect of narrative; narrative-centered structures simply use it most fully.

If we can talk about three common structures, however, we can also talk about three common types of narrative arc, and any of these arcs could also be deployed in any of these structures. I alluded to these briefly in the previous chapter, and if you weren't quite sure what we were talking about, here's a more robust description.

The most common and simplest arc, the linear narrative, is the most unifocal and for many people seems to be the easiest with which to begin. It's the structure of most mysteries and many films. It's the basic story paradigm, the one where plot (or a set of facts) dominates and unfolds chronologically, and it can be an effective storytelling model for reconfiguring academic argument into narrative because it does not require a great deal of complexity in the *structure* to do successfully. On the other hand, in stories with this structure, the *telling* (the writing) becomes more emphasized. For that reason, and despite its structural simplicity, it's actually one of the harder structures to begin with for academics.

There is also the circular quest narrative, in which a character sets out on a quest from a particular narrative location; encounters obstacles, failures, and grace; surmounts the obstacles; and returns to the place the story began, changed by the story itself. It's the

---

structure of most tragedies, but it's also an effective tool for academic narratives because it allows the researcher to demonstrate relevance (hopefully without the attendant tragedy) by narrating a quest for answers to a research question and how the quest changed the researcher (and by extension changes the reader if he or she has identified with the researcher-protagonist). This is a structure that is increasingly used in public-facing science writing, primarily because there are certain advantages to introducing the policy makers who are often the ideal audience to a research team or to a researcher. This structure typically deploys the researcher-as-character. The challenge, of course, is in transforming Dr. Jones into Indiana Jones in a way that feels — and reads as — authentic.

Finally, there's the enveloping narrative, which is a functional mix of the other two. It's also known as a frame narrative. The expansive middle of the story is a linear narrative. The beginning and the end of the narrative, however, are bracketed by a narratorial voice, which can be either the author-as-character or an internal (historical) narrator-character. So, for example, you could have a history of Pompeii, in which (assuming you had the fact-based research to support this characterization) the narrator of the frame might be a person who experienced the explosion of Vesuvius. Or the narrator could be the author-researcher, speaking as a character. Technically, it would be possible to do this in any of the voices of writing (first-person "I," second-person "you," third-person "he/she/they"). Technically, the middle of the story could be a second quest narrative rather than a linear one. What matters is that the narrator starts and ends the story, and narrator is changed in the space between those two frames. It is simply that the narrator's circular quest coincides with and is replaced by the linear narrative that constitutes the story (or is doubled if it's a circular interior narrative). It's a very effective way of telling a certain form of character-driven and embodied history.

I don't mean to suggest that these three are the only possible narrative structures. Of course, there are other, more experimental forms. There are non-linear narratives, stream-of-consciousness narratives, and the list goes on. However, these are the three typical structures, and it is not my experience that experimental or stream-of-consciousness narrative forms are useful for academics transitioning expository research into general audience narrative formats. Straight linear narratives require very tight narrative pacing at the sentence level, which in nonfiction can be difficult especially for new practitioners. Frame or enveloping narratives are probably the most useful for academics writing general audience nonfiction, as long as your interior frame has a narrative focus. Otherwise, the circular narrative is the best way to create narrative arc for material that is not inherently narrative; however, circular arcs require strong internal character development and are generally more appropriate for memoir or for nonfiction subjects where the author has access to very robust diary or memoir sources. And, for reasons my agent and I have never managed to understand satisfactorily, narratives with a single thread and also a main central protagonist seem to appeal to readers more (and therefore to sell better) than narratives in which there are several characters coming in and out of a unified story.

Whatever structure you use, I actually think it comes down to much the same thing in the end anyhow: the key is to have a pivot of some kind, a turning of attention, of tension, of modality, where the function of the pivot is to tighten or loosen tension for the reader. You can do that at the level of the sentence, at the level of narrative, or through character. Ideally, you are doing it through all three simultaneously.

This history of these narratological patterns is not, I should say, my original insight. In fact, neurolinguistic researchers would tell us that all of this is pretty well hardwired. A recent meta-data analysis of narrative form, published in the study "The Narrative Arc: Revealing Core Narrative Structures Through Text Analysis" (*Scientific Advances*, August 2020, 6:32), found "consistent patterns of narrative processes across . . . diverse cultures," and those patterns use the basic tripartite structures. According to the scientific literature, "From an evolutionary perspective, the structure of storytelling may provide a crucial way for people (or different groups) to share information." Whether it's nature or nurture, as a human species we are also now more than ten thousand years into our narrative "processes," and our cognitive and affective systems have evolved in tandem with stories that use particular conventions and structures.

There is also some interesting work done by Dr. Paul Zak, published in a study titled "Why Inspiring Stories Make Us React: The Neuroscience of Narrative" (*Cerebrum*, January–February 2015), suggesting that "inspiring stories" — in other words, stories in which a character, called on to act outside conventional limits, encounters and triumphs over conflict and obstacles — alter our brain chemistry in ways that are mutually reinforcing. "Inspiring" stories increase our levels of cortisol and oxytocin. On one hand, the chemical release facilitated by certain narrative forms leads us to be more socially empathic, perhaps underscoring the cultural efficacy of storytelling and its under-utilized potential in communications across the academic disciplines. On the other hand, the positive neurological flooding is also its own reward: oxytocin flooding the brain feels good. Stories that release oxytocin are pleasurable — and, unsurprisingly, "popular."

I don't want to over-emphasize the neurological approach. I am cognizant of the ways in which it plays into certain tendencies in the humanities, in particular, to feel the need to legitimize itself through recourse to scientific (and science-based funding) models, whether it's the technological relevance of the digital humanities or the evolutionary history of story. However, at the same time, my sense is that we also have a tendency in the humanities — and especially in literature departments, where narrative is one of the research specializations — to want to speak of narrative as a very narrow field of expertise rather than part of the essential human experience.

Chapter 5

THE ORGANIC ILLUSION OF NARRATIVE (AND HOW TO STRUCTURE A TRADE NONFICTION TITLE)

What you are looking to accomplish through this tightening and loosening of tensions, in whichever narrative structure you are working, is to create the sense that this story is weaving itself. In other words, you are trying to create the effect of an organic narrative and the sense that the story is unfolding as it must, because that is its story destiny. These are the stories that Hawthorne talked about as "spontaneous," and these are the "effective narratives" neurobiologists are studying when they talk about structures that our brains are hardwired by evolutionary biology to respond to chemically.

Of course it is not true that stories tell themselves, any more than statues emerge from stones unaided. Books do not write themselves, though professional authors with thousands of hours of experience, once certain skills become habituated, will often speak of the moment in the composition process when the narrative seems to the writer to unfold itself. It's a moment of mastery masquerading as grace, and if you ever experience it you will know.

The tightening and loosening of tension so that the unfolding and trajectory of the narrative structure seems organic and inevitable

---

is what editors mean when they talk about the narrative arc of your project. The metaphor is a different one. Imagine an arrow shot into the space and time of story. The arrow follows its own trajectory back to earth, and it appears to do so free from the hand of any archer. Of course, the moment the archer looked into the sky, took the angle of the wind and the direction of the weather, sighted the target, and pulled back the bow all invisibly shaped its flight. All of that is craft and praxis. But once the arrow flies, it appears to fly as its own creature. That is propulsive narrative. In some sense, it's another way of saying what we talked about in the section on the general audience thesis: narrative arc is a way of talking about a narrative in which the author does not get in between the story and the reader as the explainer or the mediator.

Tension can be developed both through what you say and also through what you don't say. Tension is not primarily what happens to the characters in a narrative. Tension is what the reader experiences in response to that happening. This is why over-narrating (placing yourself between the reader and the narrative) is counterproductive and why allowing the reader agency can be highly effective. A good example of dramatic tension created by a strategic absence of telling is what we all know as the cliffhanger, although there are more subtle modalities.

Character is another one of the vehicles for that tightening and loosening of tension. You will need to learn as a pragmatic matter how to develop effective character. Most simply, characters need to have both internal and external motivations, they need to have both internal and external obstacles, and they need to be individuated. The reason stereotypes and stock characters are annoying to readers is because their motivations and obstacles are not persuasive and they are not individuated. Motivation and individuation are closely connected. And, even if character is not the device used for pacing, there needs to be a character with whom the reader is invited to identify. A sentence needs a verb. A narrative needs a character.

If we were to dig down a bit deeper into how to think of narrative arc operating at the structural and functional level, I see it as a minimal pattern of certain turnings in the weaving of story. First, of course, the author has to get out of the way. For academic writers this is, once again, perhaps the critical piece of advice: get out of the way of your story. Begin from a place of narrative, not a place of exposition. If you are in your story, it had better be as a character in the story (including the option of an author-as-character). That means you, as character, need to be individuated with internal and external motivations and conflicts.

From here, I tend to think of narrative arc as a five-act drama: a beginning, a tripartite narrative structure, and an ending. The function of the beginning is to set the narrative "clock" to ticking. It's the wind-up of tension that the story will release. At its simplest this means introducing a character and a conflict or problem. The function of the ending is simple. The role of the ending is to gather the threads and to connect those gathered threads to an emotionally satisfying moment of resolution for the characters and the readers. It should feel like that clock of narrative time is winding down and clicking more and more slowly so that its stopping feels inevitable. Emotionally satisfying does not necessarily mean happy. In many history genres, especially biography, the emotionally satisfying conclusion for one's characters means narrating their death or some other ending that cannot be reopened, at least not in the frame of this story. Emotionally satisfying means either a resolution or an acceptance of the irresolvable.

The part that requires the greatest coordination is what happens in the middle three acts. My sense is that these middle three parts of a narrative, in order to create an arc, have to perform at least three separate but related functions to be effective. There has to be at least one twist, at least one false pivot, and at least one actual pivot. There can be more, sub-threads, as it were, but my sense is that there must be at least one of each, and that they do need to unfold in that order.

A twist (part two) is a moment that looks like a resolution to some starter problem, initiated in the opening, but that ends up creating a series of new conflicts and intensifications. A twist is unexpected complication. A basic story is in motion: a character, a conflict. The twist needs to be a surprise, to the reader and to the protagonist, and it's functionally the moment one thinks, "Uh oh, this is going to get interesting." If we take up that old thread metaphor, it's the first little tangle that has to be worked at a bit and loosened (though not necessarily completely untangled) before the story can move forward. For a twist to work, it needs to be far enough from the pivot (part four) to give yourself space to re-accelerate the narrative, but you also need for the initial narrative ("the beginning") already to be sufficiently under way for the twist to seem unexpected.

The false pivot (part three) can be thought of as the apparent resolution of the problem created by the initial narrative and the twist. Pivots (or climaxes) in narrative are moments when the conflict reaches a point where something must move in one direction or another that is determinative and changes the outcome. A false pivot, then, is a pivot that appears to be determinative but is revealed to be a second and generally more substantial entanglement. Both twists and false pivots function as an intensification of conflict. False pivots are moments in a narrative when the apparent resolution of

---

one aspect of the conflict is revealed to contain within it the seeds of a new and greater complication. Think of the false pivot as the "out of the frying pan, into the fire" moment in a narrative. When we talk about a false pivot containing — and being seen by the reader to contain — the seeds of a greater complication, we're talking about what an editor might call dramatic tension. When dramatic tension happens at the end of a section or at the end of a chapter, we generally use the term "cliffhanger."

The (actual) pivot (part four) is the event or change of direction that marks the beginning of the resolution. It's the climax of the narrative, where the conflicts or threads knot together tightly and the reader begins to see, as well, how all the threads will come untangled. In a big idea (accordion) narrative, it might be a movement from expansion on a thesis toward drawing together conclusions. It might be a movement from particular to abstract (or vice versa). In a biography, it is almost certainly going to be the lifetime achievement that justifies the biography, before I start the inevitable process of narrating the death of my subject.

Following this rubric, you can from here pretty easily start to block out the narrative structure of your project, and you need to do that before you can effectively write (or get started drafting) the narrative summary and chapter summaries of your book proposal.

There is one last thing, however, that you want to understand before you begin the work of outlining the narrative arc of your proposed trade topic and laying that arc out in the chapter summaries, the second central component of a book proposal: the rules of the trade nonfiction genre.

Your chapter outlines — and later, your chapters — are going to reflect certain limitations in general audience publishing. A general audience nonfiction book is, on average, eighty-five thousand words. Occasionally, there will be a preference for books as low as fifty thousand words. Only exceptionally is there a market for books with more than a hundred thousand words in trade nonfiction. You are almost certainly not going to get a contract to write a four hundred thousand word book. Books that long are outliers, the almost exclusive domain of presidential biographers, star professors, or well-established authors whose books reliably sell in the hundreds of thousands of copies.

It's worth, perhaps, saying a bit about why publishers prefer nonfiction books in the range of eighty to ninety thousand words. It is not because publishers want to read only shorter books or are assuming that audiences have only short attention spans (though that may or may not be the case). It's because of the economic realities of unit prices and publishing costs.

Bigger books simply cost more to produce, and those costs are often disproportionate when you consider the restricted profit margins in the industry. Larger books not only cost more to print and bind, requiring more paper and more pages; they also cost more to copy edit, to proofread, to clear through the legal department (a "legal read"), and to ship. Publishers sell books to retailers — everything from Amazon to your local independent bookstore — at steep discounts and on consignment, with the understanding that unsold books can be returned to the publisher. Editors are weighing a whole series of unknowns about an individual book and its sales potential and balancing their best guesses against some relatively tight business practices.

Put simply, a four hundred thousand word book, if it loses money for the press, is going to lose substantially more than an eighty thousand word book. If your eighty thousand word book does well and earns the press a profit, the profit, per unit price, will also be larger than for a four hundred thousand word book, because retail prices for thick and thin books vary only modestly. An editor would have to have a very compelling reason to believe that a high-word-count book is going to sell well in order to take that kind of gamble, and if you're a first-time general audience author, you aren't bringing to the table any sales record.

So, with all the caveats about how there are always outliers and exceptions to any rule, your proposal is best positioned to succeed if you assume your manuscript will be eighty to ninety thousand words. Two of my last three contracts, with two different publishers, have been for eighty-eight thousand words, at the publisher's particular request, apparently because that's a number that works well on the book-design side. Books, remember, are bound in signatures of sixteen pages, and publishers have in-house design parameters, as well as sales calculations. Whatever word count you agree on with a publisher, you want to keep to it within a few thousand words. That's about the limit of wiggle room for adjustments in margins and font sizes in most in-house design templates. What a publisher does not want is half a signature of empty pages, and fair's fair: trade writing is writing for contract, and the costs of production are part of what the publisher was budgeting when offering you an advance in the beginning.

If word count matters to your publisher, you also want to think about individual chapters from the reader's perspective. For general audiences, you are looking to keep your chapter lengths modest. General audience readers are not less intelligent readers or less interested readers. However, they are readers who have more diverse and frequent claims on their attention when reading than many academics, who read and research for a living. You are writing a book that someone can read for fifteen minutes in the car while waiting for a child's soccer game to end or between the jostling of seatmates on a flight. You want to keep the length of chapters roughly comparable, so those general audience readers know what to expect, and you want your readers to be able to move from chapter to chapter in a reasonable time period. You can most usefully think of the general audience reader as an informed, intelligent, and engaged person who simply happens not to be a specialist and who is likely to have demands on his or her attention.

There are also good writing reasons to keep chapters trim. Shorter chapters perform some of the important work of pacing and narrative tension. Because each chapter needs to be a satisfying unit of story, the faster those units come, the faster the pacing that a reader experiences. A good length for a chapter in a general audience nonfiction book is three thousand to five thousand words, with perhaps a shorter prologue and a shorter epilogue if you find those framing devices useful. An average reader can read about three thousand words in about ten minutes.

You need to know all of this, of course, before you start developing the chapter outlines for your book project, and you can work back on the math pretty quickly. If you have a book that's around eighty-five thousand words and you have an average chapter length of four thousand words, you're looking at a book with around twenty-one chapters, or twenty chapters plus a short prologue and a short epilogue. If your book is eighty thousand words, that's one chapter less. A few words more, a few words less, the numbers shift slightly again, but you are going to end up with somewhere between seventeen and twenty-one chapters in a typical trade nonfiction manuscript.

That means what you're looking to do at the next stage of your project development is to divide your book project into roughly twenty discrete sections, give or take a chapter or two on either side of that number. For each of these sections, you need to give a brief description. Each chapter description should be at least a few sentences. It should not be longer than a paragraph or perhaps two short paragraphs. These are your chapter-by-chapter outlines.

Writing chapter outlines requires some deft skill, and if it's your first time writing a general audience nonfiction proposal, this is a skill that may take some work to acquire and hone. I recommend reading this book to the end before starting the chapter outlines, because there is a substantial practical element. Your editor or agent is going to be looking to see whether the chapter outlines, taken as a whole, show a project that is unified in at least one of the ways we discussed in the chapter on topic development. These readers will be looking to see whether there is a big idea that remains compelling over the course of a book or whether there is character development, or how you are unifying the book, perhaps, using author-as-character. You are very likely as well to encounter an editor asking to see the narrative arc of the book—and she will want to see a narrative arc in each chapter. In other words, you're working to ensure that each chapter functions *both* to move the book as a whole forward *and* as an independent and satisfying unit.

Let's go back to my Mary Ann Patten book idea that I gave as the second example of a narrative summary. Mulling it over, I've decided I am going to work with an enveloping narrative structure. The outer narrative will be written in the first person and develop an author-as-character. The inner narrative frame will be linear and have the five parts of narrative we've been looking at. I will have a short first-person prologue and epilogue. I'll make "my" journey as narrative circular in structure, so you can see what that looks like. A circular narrative means that the narrator-character in the prologue will have to return to the place where the narrative begins in the epilogue but be changed (in terms of internal and external motivations and conflicts) by the experience of the story. It sounds complicated, but actually the hardest narratives of all to write are straight linear narratives. A more layered narrative structure opens up a lot more opportunities to manage narrative tension in a fact-based title, simply because there are more hooks on which to hang the story.

And I need somewhere around twenty chapters, right? Remember from our earlier discussion that we are looking to shape the structure of a book that is around eighty-eight thousand words and that has somewhere around twenty chapters, with around four thousand words per chapter, average.

From here, how do we now work back to develop a structure of approximately twenty chapters and write the chapter outlines? I work on the rule of thumb that the pivot in a general audience book needs to take place at about the three-quarter mark or just a bit after. That's true, as a rule of thumb, regardless of the narrative structure. In a big-idea book like *The Body Keeps the Score,* for instance, it's the transition from the case study and character-driven chapters of the first three-quarters to the takeaway lessons readers can draw from the book's argument in the last quarter or so.

I know that the climax of my story is going to be the moment Mary Ann Patten sails into San Francisco harbor in triumph (and despair) and the race that made her famous ends. The race is the central historical event that gives Mary Ann and her story the relevance I need for a general audience title. So, I am slotting "end of the race" into the space somewhere around chapter fifteen. That leaves me a few chapters at the end of book and after the clipper ship race ends to narrate the aftermath and the "rest" of Mary Ann's biography (chapters sixteen through twenty).

———

I know that at the beginning of the project (chapters one through four, perhaps?), because this is biography and the genre has certain conventions, I will need to narrate Mary Ann's life before the clipper ship race and need to set up the national and cultural history for which her individual story stands in. That leaves me at this point with eleven "open" chapters (five through fifteen), and I need to end that section (chapter fifteen) with the pivot. What I also know is that I am going to have somewhere well before chapter fifteen at least one twist and at least one false pivot. We might as easily use the terms "conflict" and "complication." Whatever terms we use, I'm just setting up here a basic three-part narrative structure that is as old as time, or at least as old as human storytelling.

For this story, a good twist is Mary Ann taking the helm of a clipper ship as the captain's wife. It's a twist that history has already set up for us. It's the hook. If it were expected that a pregnant nineteen-year-old woman would sail a two-hundred-foot-long merchant ship around Cape Horn in 1856, if there were not strong cultural reasons why this should have been impossible, there would have to be something else unexpected to make this a general audience title.

For a twist to work, I need it to be far enough from the pivot in chapter fifteen to give myself space to re-accelerate the narrative, but I also need for the narrative of the "clipper ship race" (starting in chapter five) to already be sufficiently under way for the twist to seem unexpected. That means I'm slotting in a twist (Mary Ann takes the helm) somewhere around chapter seven or eight. The ship is going to be sailing along. Something narratively is going to be happening. Something else is going to happen that is a deepening of the complication.

Then, somewhere between the twist (chapters seven and eight) and the pivot (chapter fifteen) I need to find in the research a false pivot, which is to say a moment in which there is an interim resolution, followed by an intensification and new conflict, leading to the final pivot and resolution. This can come anywhere between those two points, but if I were to begin blocking this out, I'd slot my false pivot in somewhere around chapter eleven (the midpoint). This is going to be the moment that it suddenly looks like everything is going to be, as it were, clear sailing. And then . . . Uh-oh!

I am often asked at this point by academics looking to transition to popular writing whether I'm not putting the cart before the horse. How can I decide what is going to go in chapter fifteen until I've done all my research and can make a detailed accounting of the content? Doesn't this mean that I am shaping my research around an external form? Yes, it does mean that. I am shaping the research around the form our neuroscientist peers might call effective narrative structure. But we are also fitting our research into external forms all the time, including the form of the academic monograph or the journal article when we write for academic peer audiences. Transitioning to writing for trade is simply making a genre transition.

The goal is to understand the genre of the general audience book, just as we all learned the genre of the academic article in graduate school, and then to find the places within the genre to hook our research onto that scaffolding. It does require, in my experience, a bit of toggling. You need to understand the scaffolding and hook in the first few parts of the research to establish your structure. After you've established your structure, you need to go back and do the research to begin filling out the project.

This can be a hard shift to make if you are coming from an academic background. To reiterate: you should not write your entire manuscript and then try to summarize it in a book proposal. You do not need to complete all of the research for a general audience book

---

now. Don't worry. That will come. But later. You need to start with scaffolding and do just the amount of research that is needed to write the book proposal. Then you toggle.

Start with a conventional narrative structure if you're new to this kind of writing. This is not experimental poetry. This is not a French New Wave film. You do not need to reinvent the genre. Accept that there are certain economic limitations in the world of book publishing that will dictate the length and structure of a marketable conventional narrative structure. Set down some placeholders that reflect the particular type of nonfiction you're working in (and those placeholders aren't as different as you might think), and from there, do whatever additional research you need to fill in the interstices and come up with a complete set of chapter outlines.

The particular structural placeholders that I recommend? To recap: a twist, a false pivot, and the pivot. Put the pivot at about the three-quarters mark. Yes, this does mean that you want to be looking actively in your research at this stage for how you can identify conflict, tension, resolution, surprises. You need to draw out of the research the pivot, twist, and false pivot. You need to match up the history and the data to the conventions of effective narrative communication.

I also tend to think at this stage about how to identify at least two enveloping narratives — in other words, at least two (and often three) story frames. In Falk's *Light Ages*, for example, there is the frame of "the story of medieval science." Inside that, however, there is the frame of "the story of a particular Benedictine monk." The inner (character) story of my draft proposal is "Mary Ann Patten, at the helm in a gale off Cape Horn, fighting off mutiny." That takes place within the intermediate (plot) frame of this project: "The clipper ship race of *Neptune's Car* from June–November 1856 and Mary Ann Patten's maritime adventure." In terms of this being a general audience title, the intermediate frame is the narrow part of my "narrow to broad" movement. (The inner story is the affective and inspiring story, meant to get your oxytocin going.) The exterior frame of this project is actually two frames that are overlapping each other. One frame is the generic conventions of biography (born, live, die, in chronological time), and I am working to match that up with my big-idea frame. That frame is, again, broadly, "Mary Ann Patten's experience in an 1856 clipper ship race was part of a constitutive cultural narrative about adventure, globalism, and the speed of transmission that tells us something important about the founding of the American project and about the perils of the world we live in today." And, contained in all of this is the simple economic reality that I need a book of about eighty-five thousand words and about twenty, roughly equal, chapters.

When it's time to sit down to start hammering out the chapter outlines (and expect a lot of back-and-forth editing and revision here while you find a structure that feels organic), it is with this narrative structure in mind: prologue (stage setting); chapters one through four (wind-up, external frame); chapters five through seven (wind-up, internal frame); chapters seven to eight (twist); chapters nine to ten (intensification of internal frame); chapter eleven (false pivot); chapters twelve through fourteen (climax and wind down of internal frame); chapter fifteen (pivot; internal-frame resolution); chapters sixteen through nineteen (wind down, external frame); epilogue.

My chapter summaries might end up looking something like this:

> Prologue. First-hand account of author: author's interest in
> Mary Ann Patten's maritime story, and following in Patten's

footsteps through the Strait of Lemaire and to Antarctica. Introduces the book as adventure narrative and American history, set against climate change and the quickly disappearing ice of Antarctica. [Part of my "author platform" for this book project is that, as a sailor myself, I will make the passage around Cape Horn, at a crucial moment (climate change) in the history of that passage, as part of the research. More on the "author platform" later.]

Chapter 1. Early lives of Joshua Patten (Rockland, Maine) and Mary Ann Brown (Boston, Massachusetts), framed to tell the larger story of nineteenth-century maritime families: the allures and dangers of the great clipper races, the role of Masonic societies in the "fraternal Atlantic," and the scourge of the "White Death," tuberculosis. Culminates with the marriage of Joshua and Mary Ann and sees them departing on their first voyage, to San Francisco and then on to China, just as the California Gold Rush is reshaping the world of maritime merchants.

Chapter 2. Chapter opens in Manhattan. The Pattens have returned from China and their first trip round the Horn, and Mary Ann (nineteen) has spent the months at sea learning celestial navigation. Back at home, Joshua (twenty-five) has been tapped by the company Foster and Nickerson of New York to captain one of their fastest clippers, *Neptune's Car,* on a second voyage. The ship is docked and preparing for the new clipper race to San Francisco. The prize, if they can win the race, is a small fortune for both the captain (Joshua Patten) and the ship's owners. The route, though, is through what is still considered some of the most treacherous sailing in the world: around Cape Horn and past the Antarctic. The ship's crew is worn out, but Joshua can't resist the challenge and agrees to take the helm. Just as they are preparing for the race to begin, his trusted first mate shatters his leg, and Joshua will need to decide whether to give in to pressure from the ship's owners and take on board a new first mate, William Keeler.

——

Chapter 3. Joshua has misgivings. But the prize money and the adventure are too great a temptation. Chapter opens on the morning the clipper ship race is set to begin. There are four clippers vying to reach San Francisco first. Crowds line the docks of Manhattan to see the beginning of what was celebrated as a cultural event in the city, and *Neptune's Car* is towed to anchor to wait for the starting guns and the tide. It's July first, and the weather is oppressively humid and hot, leading to short tempers. Despite old salts whispering that a woman was bad luck on a voyage, Mary Ann Patten is again making the trip as the captain's wife. Worse: this captain's wife was also, whether she knew it yet or not, two months pregnant. Chapter closes with the starting guns. The race has started, and the bookmakers in New York City have Joshua Patten as the favorite to win. They hope to make San Francisco in one hundred days.

Chapter 4. Tensions aboard ship and the first signs of Captain Patten's illness as they make their way — racing the other three clippers — down the Eastern Seaboard, past the Caribbean, and along the east coast of South America into the South Atlantic Ocean. They cross the equator on July 27th in light winds. Chapter introduces the main characters among the crew and the strange and dangerous events that keep taking place on board the ship (with a bit of sailing context for readers who may be unfamiliar). Someone is trying to sabotage the journey, and, in the captain's quarters at night, Joshua and Mary Ann are increasingly convinced that the ringer first mate, Keeler, is the problem. Privately, there are also growing concerns that Joshua is seriously unwell — and unease about how to hide this weakness from Keeler.

Chapter 5. Dramatic and dangerous events continue aboard *Neptune's Car*, and matters come to a head on ship when the increasingly insolent first mate is caught red-handed. Captain Patten exercises rough maritime justice and, at gunpoint, orders the furious and still scheming first mate confined below decks to his cabin. Not everyone on the crew supports the captain. There was an old saying in the 1850s about the latitudes they are now entering: "Beyond forty degrees south there is no law. Beyond fifty degrees south there is no God." Sometimes the crew noted that the captain seemed muddled, and the ship nearly went down off the Falkland Islands when a sleet storm at sea tossed it sideways. Was he really going to wreck them all, as Keeler kept muttering? Some of the crew members were starting to wonder. They were also unhappy that the captain made William Hare, a brutish man, the replacement first mate. The third mate, George Kingsley, is also proving to be a troublemaker.

Chapter 6. Approach to the Straits of Lemaire, some of the most dangerous waters in the world. Icebergs float in the narrow straits, where the currents toss boats wildly. There are legends of a "ghost ship" — a mirage of wet, black rocks that ruined captains soft-hearted enough to try to help fellow mariners in trouble. Chapter looks at the other ships in the race (*Intrepid; Romance of the Seas; Invincible*) and narrative history of Antarctica's role in nineteenth-century maritime trade. By the time the race boats are approaching the fifty-degree parallel, they realize something sobering: they are sailing too early in the season. The ship's owners have pressed for the race to take place as soon as the weather permits. But in Antarctica it's unseasonably cold, and the two previous winters had pressed the ice farther north than usual. And just as they come into the most perilous part of the passage, where currents can easily toss a clipper against rock cliffs in freezing waters, Joshua collapses. There is no turning back.

Chapter 7. Near mutiny aboard ship. The captain is delirious and now in and out of consciousness. Following the incarceration of Keeler, Hare had been moved into the crucial role as first mate. But Hare cannot read and so cannot navigate them safely though the waters. The crew begins to debate unshackling Keeler, and Mary Ann is afraid that he will shipwreck them or sail off course to throw the race, which she is still determined to win. She's also afraid he will harm Joshua. Working from just her good sense, seamanship, and books in Joshua's captain's library, Mary Ann makes a bold decision: She will take the helm. She knows how to read and how to navigate. In a dramatic showdown with the crew, she declares herself captain. The crew, uncertain, is moved by her determination and courage and unanimously votes to support her at the helm.

Chapter 8. Mary Ann at the helm. This is Patagonia, where the Pacific and the Atlantic meet in a vast tumbling of water, current, and winds. They pass the Straits of Lemaire, but as they enter the open waters near False Cape Horn a terrible gale slammed into them. This area can experience tremendous storms because of the geography, which funnels the winds known as the "williwaws" through Drake's Passage. *Neptune's Car* is groaning and shuddering under the impact of the waves and winds. Mary Ann and the crew know that dozens of vessels have shipwrecked here. Sailors who have passed the Horn were allowed by tradition to wear a gold earring—gold so if their bodies washed up their families could afford the funeral. Mary Ann realizes the ship cannot survive the night and will go down unless she can find a way to escape the storm.

Chapter 9. Mary Ann makes the only decision she can: to turn and run downwind, to be blown backward, out of the storm. And blown straight into polar Antarctica. The skies are too clouded to navigate by the stars, so she will have to sail by "dead reckoning." The sailors aboard knew another saying: If there was no law in the "roaring forties" and no God in the "furious fifties," in the "screaming sixties" there was no hope. Antarctica had only been discovered in the early nineteenth century. The first charts were not printed until 1820. The continent remained a terrifying terra incognita for all but the most intrepid adventurers. Chapter recounts the harrowing story of that night aboard *Neptune's Car*, and the realization on the other side of the storm that their troubles are only just beginning.

Chapter 10. Escape from Antarctica. Sailors who entered Antarctic waters would later talk of the other-worldliness they saw. Icebergs towered above them, and a thick fog settled in. They would have to sail by sound for parts of the journey in order to avoid collision. Mary Ann and her crew are exhausted, Joshua remains incoherent and delirious, they are in dangerous water, and they need to navigate — without the aid of modern technology — back on course. And Mary Ann wants, too, to make up for lost time on the race to San Francisco.

Chapter 11. It would take them another fifty days aboard *Neptune's Car* to make up lost ground and navigate past the infamous Cape Horn, a massive cliff face. It was a storied landscape: they pass the island that inspired *Robinson Crusoe*. During those fifty days, Mary Ann refused to leave the helm or even to change her clothing, working nearly around the clock with Hare and the crew to steer the ship to safer waters. When they finally pass the cape, a cheer goes up. They are past the worst, and even the captain seems to be showing some signs of recovering.

Chapter 12. The worst is past and the ship has survived, but they have lost time in the race, and a fortune is at stake — along with her husband's reputation. Mary Ann, whose pregnancy is now showing, is shattered from the exertion, and Joshua, lucid and appearing to make a recovery, persuades her to unshackle a repentant Keeler and allow Keeler and Hare to manage the crew under his convalescent supervision. It should be smooth sailing to California from here, and perhaps they can still win the race prize. Mary Ann agrees to Keeler's release, but reluctantly; she still doesn't trust the first mate and something is niggling at her. Within days, continuing to carefully chart their course in secret, she discovers that Keeler is steering the vessel off course — not for San Francisco but right for Valparaiso — a port town on the western coast of South America. He is once again trying to throw the race. Mary Ann reveals the betrayal to Joshua. Keeler is once again hauled off below decks, to await punishment once they land in California.

Chapter 13. Joshua collapses again from the strain, sinking at first into blindness and then a coma, and Mary Ann once more takes the helm. They are near Santiago, but they still need to pass Mexico, and then the southern coast of California. Flurry aboard ship as gear is checked and organized. Everyone knows about the Gold Rush and wants to stake a claim — or just sell a product. The winds were steady for the last weeks of the journey up the coast. They cross back over the equator just before mid-September, a hundred and three days out of New York City. By now, they are traveling the North Pacific in the autumn storm season, and they are hit by gales off Point Conception, near Santa Barbara, only to be becalmed for more than a week in stifling temperatures on the other side of the weather system. Mary Ann, six months pregnant, navigates on November 14th past the treacherous islands known as the Devil's Teeth (today: Farralon), just thirty miles from San Francisco harbor. From there, a tug will come to tow the clipper into port the next morning. Down below, still in chains, Keeler is determined to make his escape. When *Neptune's Car* lands, he will be arrested and charged with mutiny.

Chapter 14. On November 15, 1856 — one hundred thirty-six days after leaving New York City — *Neptune's Car* was towed into San Francisco harbor, with Mary Ann and William Hare at the helm. The crew erupts in jubilation. All the crew, that is, except Keeler, who, with the help of third mate Kingsley, has slipped his shackles and jumps over the side just as the ship comes into harbor. It has been a harrowing voyage, and their competitor, *Romance of the Seas*, had beaten them to the first prize, arriving a full three weeks earlier. But, despite it all, they had still taken second place in the race. Given all that they have suffered, not being dead last was a triumph. But there is a sober tone on the helm: Joshua is deathly ill. Little do the crew or the captain's wife know that already word was spreading across San Francisco. Was it true, people asked in the harbor, that the captain's pregnant nineteen-year-old wife had taken them around Cape Horn in a terrible storm?

Chapter 15. News spreads in San Francisco of the astonishing story of *Neptune's Car*. Press converges at the docks. Mary Ann Patten, already a media sensation, steps onto the docks to applause. The crowd falls silent as Joshua is carried off in a litter. The chapter recounts scenes of San Francisco during the heyday of the Gold Rush and the story of Mary Ann's battle just beginning with the ship's owners over her husband's payment.

Chapter 16. Joshua makes a slow and modest recovery in California, where the ship's owners failed to support the captain financially but where Mary Ann's international celebrity finally resulted in the press and his Masonic Lodge back east raising enough money to send Joshua to a hospital. The ship's owners are declining to pay his salary of five thousand dollars, on the grounds that he was incapacitated during the voyage. Mary Ann makes the final decision in January 1857 to travel overland and by steam-ship back from San Francisco to Boston via Panama (where no canal yet existed), a two-month journey, to return home to support and family. For merchant sailors, only the opening of the Panama Canal in 1914 would relieve the terrors of Cape Horn, which were the stuff of sea lore for more than three hundred years, from the moment of its discovery as a trade-route passage.

Chapter 17. The story of Mary Ann Patten's astonishing feat—because dead reckoning through a gale off Cape Horn and living to tell the tale remains, even today, an astonishing feat of seamanship—did not end back in Boston. In the spring of 1857, following the birth of a baby boy in March and the progress of Joshua's illness, now confirmed as the "White Plague," tuberculosis, the story of *Neptune's Car* remained an international headline. There is renewed interest when Mary Ann agrees to give detailed interviews. There is press coverage of Mary Ann as a heroine in London, New York, across America, as well as national outrage at the continued withholding of Joshua's salary. Readers begin fundraising to support the "captain's wife" and the "Florence Nightingale of the Seas," and there is a public campaign to shame the insurers and ship owners into awarding Mary Ann a lump sum. After all, through her efforts, three hundred thousand dollars of insured cargo — a figure worth some sixty million dollars in today's values — was saved from certain destruction. Back in San Francisco, *Neptune's Car* remained at dock, and by now the violent third mate George Kingsley had jumped ship, like William Keeler before him, charged with murder of another crew member.

Chapter 18. Then, of course, the story faded. The public had moved on by the time Joshua died — completely insensible and out of his mind from the late stages of meningitis induced by the tuberculosis in late July at an asylum in Boston. When Joshua passed away, the world press might not have been watching, but all of Boston's maritime community was. Bells tolled in the harbor as the news of Captain Patten's death spread and flags on the clippers in the harbor were lowered to half mast, but it was by now a local story. And no one in the press covered the awful and inevitable consequence of Mary Ann's nursing her husband: by late 1857, she too had contracted tuberculosis at his bedside.

Chapter 19. Afterlife of Mary Ann Patten. Her death from tuberculosis in the spring of 1861; the unhappy fate of their orphaned son, sent to live with family in Rockport, Maine. The world that Mary Ann and Joshua inhabited lasted only a decade or two. Gold had been discovered in 1848. By 1869, the last golden spike driven into the ground in Utah heralded the opening of the transcontinental railway, which would make long-distance sea travel — and extreme clipper-ship races — increasingly unnecessary. There would come the opening of the Panama Canal a few decades later, and by then only adventurers or great cargo ships would attempt to transit

Cape Horn, not small-time merchant sailors. A few times in the intervening century and a half, the story of Mary Ann Patten would drift back into public consciousness. The suffragettes would claim her as an icon in their quest for women's civil rights. The Merchant Marine Academy would commemorate her seamanship as an inspiration to all of its professional sailors. But mostly history went silent.

Epilogue. If the story of Mary Ann Patten and the world she inhabited only lasted a decade or two longer, having come into being as a result of the combined historical forces of the clipper races, the tuberculosis epidemic, and the California Gold Rush, the Antarctic waters that she navigated on that voyage might also be with us only a short period longer. With climate change in our moment, the trade winds are shifting—and this time those trade winds are not metaphoric. First-person final chapter, placing Mary Ann's story in the context of more contemporary global races for the supply chain and more contemporary pandemics.

What you can see is that the threads of the narrative structure in these sample chapters are quite carefully interwoven and paced. I mentioned above thinking of this structure as having at least two narratives. In fact, while these chapter outlines have two narratives, there are at least five separate narrative strands, with character as the hinge strand:

1. The climate change "race" and disappearance of historical Antarctica (contemporary relevance, author-as-character frame, prologue/epilogue). Relevance (contemporary thesis).

2. The clipper "race" (*Neptune's Car* versus the other ships) and its thematic/thesis stand-ins (globalism, colonialism, exploration, pandemic). Relevance (historical thesis).

———

3. The conflict between captain and company (a stand-in for the internal character conflict Joshua struggles with, safety versus fortune). Narrative (historical).

4. The conflict between captain(s) and crew, focused primarily on Joshua and Mary Ann versus Keeler. Character (bridging historical and contemporary central narrative focus in biography, and genre expectations).

5. The conflict between humans and nature and geography (Cape Horn). Narrative (both historical and contemporary).

Looking at the structure of this proposed title, and from the fact that character is the hinge between narratives (and narratives are doing the work of building the big idea), what I know is that, although this book has strong central characters, this is primarily a narrative-driven book. Historical events are driving the story. Mary Ann Patten is a character who rose to a historical challenge.

Is this likely to be my final draft? Probably not. There are a few things as I go further that I will want to fiddle with — things that you may also find yourself doing and wanting to double-check yourself on. What are my concerns? Well, I'm concerned that what's big about this story is maybe getting sidelined a bit by my desire to get the facts down on paper and lay out a timeline. That's natural. I'm trying to wrestle with history and narrative and some genre limitations and slot some things into place, and I've over-emphasized here so you get the idea how the narrative tension and chapter movements are working, probably slightly to the detriment of character. After all, we haven't got to characterization yet. But in my final revision, I'll want to be sure to edit out some of that scaffolding. I'll want to focus on capturing characters in a phrase to make them pop. I'll want to delineate a bit more narrowly the different story lines and move all this toward organic story.

In fact, as things actually played out with this book proposal, which sold at auction in July 2023, I did ultimately find a bigger frame for this story that also helped deepen characterization, and I decided to address these nagging concerns by revising the narrative overview rather than the chapter summaries. I decided that was the best way to hit the high notes I wanted to emphasize, in the place where they were likely to get the most attention. In the final revision, this is what I ended up with as an updated narrative summary:

> A new contribution to Antarctic extreme adventure and women's historical biography from Tilar J. Mazzeo, author of the *New York Times* bestselling *Widow Clicquot, Irena's Children, Hotel on Place Vendôme*, etc.
>
> Set in the summer of 1856 in the midst of a celebrity clipper ship race to deliver supplies to the California Gold Rush and in the midst of the mid-nineteenth-century tuberculosis epidemic, captain's wife Mary Ann Patten is forced to take the helm, put down a mutiny, and attempt to steer a two-hundred-foot clipper ship laden with the modern equivalent of sixty million dollars of cargo through Drake's Passage and around Cape Horn, the most treacherous waters in the world. Caught in an eighteen-day gale, with her husband sick and unconscious, Mary Ann makes the only choice she can to save the ship and her crew and turns to run out of the storm and straight into Antarctic waters. In doing so she becomes both the first woman to command a merchant vessel and among the first women to navigate through the dangerous and magical landscape of Antarctica.
>
> How did Patten accomplish what no woman had done before — and what even seasoned male captains today (including the U.S. Merchant Marine Academy) consider an astonishing feat of seamanship? It's also an untold story of how national crowd-sourcing and big data transformed American commerce and the lives of women like Patten.

———

To navigate the most treacherous waters in the world in an era before satellites and cell phones, a sailor needed three things: a watch (invented in the mid-seventeenth century), a sextant (invented in the mid-eighteenth century), and nautical charts, which in the 1840s were still unreliable. Until a technocrat civil servant in the U.S. hydrological service named Matthew Maury decided to mine old ships' logs for data and asked a captain to try to sail by the data as an experiment. When the captain cut the time of the journey by twenty percent on the first try, sea captains and the commercial world went wild for a grassroots movement to participate in the discovery. Captains — including a young Captain Joshua Patten — eagerly sent their logbook data to Maury, who aggregated the data. The result: in the 1850s, for the first time, modern, scientific nautical charts were printed.

Before those charts, only a seasoned sea captain with experience and local knowledge could hope to take the helm and survive. Maury's big-data charts were a great equalizer. They made it possible for Mary Ann Patten, armed with just a good education and her intelligence and courage, to break through the ultimate nineteenth-century glass ceiling. When the story of her feat broke in newspapers internationally, she became a celebrity icon as famous as Maury himself, and in the decade after her groundbreaking voyage a half dozen other women famously took the helm as sea captains. Today, the U.S. government continues to produce the state-of-the-art nautical charts that Maury pioneered, but the story of how a previously faceless technocrat and a nineteen-year-old woman brought America together in our first national citizen-science achievement has not yet been told. It is also a timely reminder of how access to science, education, and data can transform the lives of individuals and nations.

Drawing on the author's first-hand expedition in 2022 to Antarctica in search of Patten's route, as well as new archival research into nineteenth-century women's maritime journals and the Maury logbooks in the Library of Congress, this adventurous narrative

---

biography is a timely contribution to new and increasingly relevant travel writing about the White Continent and its climate history.

This project has been supported by funding from the National Endowment for the Humanities (2022–2023).

That was the final narrative summary as it went out for contract. It also served its purpose. There ended up being a four-way best-bids auction on the project based on this narrative summary, these chapter summaries, and the remainder of the proposal; the book went under contract with a very nice deal at a Big Five imprint. Even with that said, the final book will probably bear only a passing relation to the details in the last iteration of the book proposal. The purpose of the book proposal is to get a trade contract. Once you sign that contract, you are bound in a general way to deliver the title proposed, but no one in the industry expects that the project won't evolve, perhaps significantly, in dialogue with your editor.

Chapter 6

THE BOOK PROPOSAL (AND CAVEAT ENTREPRENEUR)

You have found a general audience topic. You have a narrative summary, and maybe now you even have chapter outlines. If so, you have the first two sections of a book proposal drafted. Let's step back and talk about some of the realities of publishing general audience nonfiction, including the central role of the book proposal in what comes next, so you can begin to plan how to draft the rest of the document.

There is some important and excellent news for academics looking to secure a nonfiction trade contract, as we've already said: you do not need to draft the entire manuscript. In fact, you should not draft the entire manuscript. The final shape of your book will be the result of a series of conversations and, if things are working well, collaborations between you and your editor, and, especially if you are writing your first general audience book, there will be some specific features of the writing that you are unlikely to be able to anticipate. What you need is a polished and effective complete book proposal.

We have already drafted here together the first two sections of a book proposal and looked at how you can toggle between them to

---

lay out a narrative arc and hone a narrative summary that develops story. As you have seen, the goal of the first is to pitch your book idea as a general audience topic that is big: big enough to have ten thousand or more waiting reader-buyers. The goal of the second is, ostensibly, to outline how that book develops and what it will contain. But the more crucial goal of the chapter outlines is to show that you know how to work with narrative and not just narration.

There are three other sections of the book proposal we'll want to consider: a market-analysis section; an author-platform, audience, and marketing section; and a sample chapter. But let's start with the basics.

A book proposal is going to run somewhere on the order of eight to twelve thousand words. The publishing industry deals in word counts rather than number of pages for the simple reason that, as every student who has ever experimented with font size knows, page counts are highly variable. But in general, we're talking around thirty to fifty double-spaced pages, or fifteen to twenty-five single-spaced pages.

The first page of your book proposal, your cover sheet, will be your title, your name as author, and the name and contact address of your agent. We will talk more about how to propose a title a little further on in this chapter, and you will need a complete book proposal before you can reasonably approach an agent.

The second page of your book proposal is a table of contents, and, again, the contents of your book proposal are going to include the following sections: a narrative summary; chapter outlines; a market analysis; a section on author platform, the projected audience, and author contributions to marketing; and a sample chapter.

You can customize the names of these sections, and you can rearrange the order of them as well if you feel strongly. You can divide the last section into a series of smaller sections if you would rather. There are as many ways to write a great book proposal as there are individual book topics. But in the end, your book proposal needs to include all of these components, however you package or organize them. There are also some relatively fixed parameters for what these components need to look like and what work they need to perform.

Your narrative summary is a succinct overview of your book idea that showcases your topic as a general audience title. We've already discussed this section, but by way of a recap: a reasonable range is three to eight hundred words; five hundred words would be a good target. My final narrative summary was six hundred words, and the first and last paragraphs of that summary are my hitting a couple of author-platform notes that as a first-time trade author you may not have available. Anything longer than eight hundred words, though, isn't succinct and isn't a summary. Perhaps the most important thing in drafting your narrative summary, apart from trying to tick as many of the general audience topic boxes discussed in the previous chapter, is to resist the temptation to offer too much detail. Your goal in this summary is to include only content that serves the purpose of demonstrating the broad appeal and marketability of your project.

In the chapter outlines, your primary goals are to lay out the narrative arc of your story, and to show that you understand how to fit that story and your historical material into trade writing, with a narrative to each chapter, a narrative to the whole, and the tightening and loosening of tension and pacing. Each chapter outline is a paragraph, maybe two, so around one or two hundred words is a good target length.

We've already hinted at the role of comparative and competing titles in a market analysis when we were looking at big idea development. Your goal in this section is to show that there are no competing titles that make your proposed book a non-starter, and to show that there is sales evidence that similar titles, aimed at a similar audience, have recently been successful. I usually address in the market-analysis section the question of access to the fact-based research needed to complete this project, because I tend to think of the market analysis as the part of the wedding ceremony where the preacher asks whether anyone knows of any impediment to this marriage. For me this is the practical section of the proposal where I address any obstacles, attempt to remove stumbling blocks, and clear the path with well-chosen, timely, successful comps in one fell swoop, so from here on out the focus can be on just my proposed title.

That's an overview of the remaining components of the trade book proposal. Let's look a bit more carefully at how we choose good comps. Comparative titles are one of the ways that agents and publishers look for an author to demonstrate a market — and one of the ways that publishers build profit-and-loss projections when considering your title for an advance contract.

Your comps need to be carefully selected. You are essentially looking to identify a number of books (three or four is a good target) that are similar to your proposed title and likely to be purchased by the same demographic of readers and that recently sold in numbers substantial enough to suggest that your title might justify comparably optimistic sales projections. What are similar titles? This is probably the most difficult part of choosing comps. Remember that what matters, ultimately, is identifying an existing market of eager book buyers who already purchased a title that was similar — but not the same — as your project.

The place to start is with genre. The trade publishing market depends a fair bit on categorization and genre. Genres and sub-genres have more importance than you might think. They will materially affect, among other things, where in a bookstore your title is ultimately displayed and how it is marketed, including how the cover is designed. Different genres also have different sales demographics, some of which vary substantially in terms of the gender or the age of the average buyer. Fact-based titles, like the ones we're talking about in this book, are going to fall under the broad umbrella of adult nonfiction, but within adult nonfiction there are a number of sub-genres. The largest categories for research-based books are history, biography, memoir, travel/adventure, true crime, religion/spirituality, psychology/self-help, science, education, leadership, and current affairs/politics, although there are others. Within those categories, and especially in history, there are numerous other sub-genres.

The easiest way to visualize where your book's target market might be positioned is, again, to take a tour of a large commercial bookstore to see how sales categories are arranged. Notice which categories are given the prime real estate and which are tucked in the back of the store, where you have to hunt for them. Then think about where you'd like to see your book placed and what books you see on the shelves that have something in common with your title. Be aware that books on the front tables are there not because of genre but because those are paid placements. Generally, table books are books that are selling more briskly or books that had higher projected sales, so the tables are not bad places to look. Ending up there, however, was not an accident.

As you wander, start adding books to your list of possible comps. Ideally, your book should be able to fit comfortably into three (or more) sub-categories. For example, Candace Millard's *River of the Gods* (Doubleday, 2022), an adult nonfiction title that I am looking at in my comp researches for the Mary Ann Patten project, I notice is listed on the back cover as travel, history, and adventure/exploration for its sub-genres.

Once you have your three genre categories and some initial ideas, it's time to do some more in-depth research back at home to see if you can come up with a list of other recent books in each of those same categories that have something in common with your proposed title. The emphasis here is on recent. A number of the editors I spoke with in the process of writing this book stressed this point. Most editors want books published in the last three years, four years at the very outside. Anything published more than a few years ago does not reflect current market trends or sales demographics. It's all right to mention one or two older titles that orient a reader to the genre and sales potential, but you have to follow that up with several very recent titles that show that the market continues to be present.

Editors also told me that one of their other pet peeves in book proposals is comps that are unrealistically aspirational. If you are proposing a book that is a trade title that can support projected sales of thirty thousand copies, choosing a title as a comp that sold three million copies does not offer useful data, and it signals to a publishing house that either you or your agent don't understand the market. Understanding the market is key to lending credibility to a marketing plan.

In this section of the book proposal you want to place your title in the context of other, similar, very recent books that have sold well—as well as or better than a reasonable threshold for your project. That threshold has to be at or above the numbers your trade press considers entry level. So if you're pitching a book to a Big Five publisher, you are looking for titles that have sold at least thirty thousand copies, and it would probably be wise to look for comps that sold somewhere closer to seventy thousand copies — around the number that adds up to that "sweet spot" advance of a hundred thousand dollars. If you're a first-time author, that's probably a bit aspirational, but it's not so aspirational as to be impossible. If you're pitching a book to an independent press, the number might be ten thousand copies for comps. The key objective is to find the right match for your project and then identify comps that are strong enough and just aspirational enough to be a reach for the title. And remember that not all books are Big Five books. There are many excellent, successful books that reach a smaller but still broad general audience and are published in the other thirty percent of the trade book sector.

In fact, let's say more about that other thirty percent of the market. It is perfectly reasonable to decide that you might not want to publish a Big Five title and that you'd be happy with something much more modest than a *New York Times* bestseller. It's perfectly reasonable, in other words, to decide that you want to publish a "biggish" book, one that might be a bit more niche but one that is still aimed at a more general audience than an academic monograph and where the sales figures are in the range of five thousand copies and the advances are well under ten thousand dollars. These are entry-level trade books, positioned in the more independent part of the publishing market, and they can be both satisfying and easier places to start than a large contract. If you are looking to place a book longer than a hundred thousand words, need a longer timeline for delivery than a year or two, and are willing — and able — to accept a far more modest advance in order to complete the research and writing, smaller publishers are often able to be more flexible.

The caveat, of course, is that these entry-level books carry with them all the risks of writing for trade in the academic context and require just the same effort to execute, without the financial or platform rewards of a larger deal, which at least offers some consolation should your dean refuse to count your trade title toward merit. However modest, however niche, these are still trade titles, so the fundamental advice and general audience writing skills needed don't change either. The topic can be a bit more targeted, but that's the only difference. You still want character and a narrative arc. You still need to write that same book proposal, that same sample chapter. You still want current comps that show that, even if the market is less capacious, there is still a market.

When it comes to those comps, BookScan is the industry standard. You or your agent will want to pull these numbers before you submit a final book proposal for circulation, because an editor is going to check those figures. The BookScan subscription is expensive, however, so you may want to begin by searching Amazon and the bestseller lists and paying to search just a small number of final titles on BookScan at the end of the process by tracking and researching your comps on their monthly subscription service. Or, if you're working with an agent, agents will have a subscription to the service and can check those figures for you during the revision stage of your work together. You absolutely should expect that an agent will work with you on revising your book proposal as a final step to circulation.

Amazon sales rankings are such a moving target that they are useful only in the most generic ways, but if you search for books in broad genre categories ("history"), books that rank in the top one thousand sales positions tend to have sold broadly. Likewise, anything that was on a bestseller list (including the extended list) in any major market is likely to have sold well enough to work as a good comp. You probably aren't looking for the titles that spent thirty weeks as a number one *New York Times* bestseller. Those are likely to be unrealistically aspirational. But a title that appeared once on the *New York Times* bestseller list or for a few weeks on the extended (beyond top ten) list is a good bet to have sold respectably. Don't forget either that, although the *New York Times* is the most influential of the lists, it's not the only one or even the one that gives you the most information. Be sure to check as well the bestseller lists on the West Coast, especially the *Los Angeles Times* and *San Francisco Chronicle* lists. Those are also large and important markets for book sales. If you are looking to place titles in other English-speaking markets outside the United States, where New York City still dominates, then you'll want to check those national lists.

Whatever your market, from among books that sold well, you are searching for books that are intuitively comparable to yours. You are helping a publisher (and eventual book buyers) identify the preexisting market for your title. There are two thought exercises I tend to use in thinking about this: the first is, "A reader who liked [X title] will like this book"; the second is "This book is a cross between [X title] and [Y title]." X and Y titles are always going to be obvious commercial successes and have obvious genre or topic overlap, so the connection is intuitive to a publisher or agent. A good rule of thumb is that, if you have to explain the connection in any detail, it's not intuitive.

Competing titles are somewhat trickier. Be sure you do this research carefully — an editor will — and if there are competing titles, think about how to position them honestly. If there are other books on the same subject as your proposed title, you need to tackle that head on. Unless you are writing about some completely new discovery, it would be strange if there has never been a trade book on a related topic. If you are publishing the new, cutting-edge Shakespeare biography, it would be strange if there had never been a trade title on

Shakespeare and also never been a trade title on Renaissance drama. Publishers are wary of there being no adjacent titles. What if that's because no one is interested in that topic and there simply is no market? You are trying to find the balance between writing a trade book that is fresh and new — and writing a trade book that fits easily into an already well established book sales market.

One of the things that can worry a publisher if you have a great general audience topic and there has never been a book on the topic is whether the reason is because there is not enough historical material. Why there has never been a trade nonfiction book on this amazing event or idea or person is also a legitimate question and one that, if relevant, you want to answer as well in your book proposal. Part of what a publisher wants to know is that you understand the nonfiction contract. The nonfiction contract is clear, and unforgiving: as an author you are allowed to use all of the narrative strategies of fiction and storytelling, but you are not permitted to fictionalize or invent anything in the content.

If there has been another bestselling book on this topic, what new, compelling, and timely research is there (and how long has it been) to suggest there is space for a new title? If there has been another book on this topic — if you're proposing a new biography of William Shakespeare, and the last one was published seven years ago — there has to be something demonstrably new either in your material or in your argument and angle to make a publisher believe that those same people who bought that last Shakespeare biography and going to purchase a new one. Likewise, if there have been other general audience books on the topic and they did not sell well, is there any reason to believe the market has changed?

If that last Shakespeare biography sold poorly, by the same token, is there a reason to believe there has been a sudden upswell of interest in Shakespeare, such that people who did not purchase that one are now ready to click "buy" for this one? Is there some clear reason to believe that Shakespeare is newly relevant or timely? Resist the temptation in these cases to explain in your proposal that the last trade biography of Shakespeare was an unintelligent book or badly written. That all may be true. It doesn't really matter. If there was a previous trade book on the same topic as your proposed book, anywhere in the last fifteen years, and that book sold poorly, you have a tall mountain to climb.

Previously self-published books on the topic, which it is generally accepted do not have strong marketing or distribution channels, will generally not be held against a prospective book proposal if those titles did not sell well. Likewise, as we've noted earlier, although prior academic books on a topic are worth noting, they are not considered either comparable or competing titles for a trade book.

If you do find yourself in the situation of proposing a genuinely new book on an unexplored topic — and it does happen — just be sure that you include in your book proposal a paragraph or two outlining where the historical and archival materials are located and giving a reasonable explanation of why you're confident of being able to access them. As an academic, you will generally have unrestricted access to all publicly or institutionally held materials, as long as they are not under collection restrictions, but in some cases corporate or private documents are more complex, and publishers just want to know that you've thought through the materials.

That leaves only one other topic to cover in this section: identification of the reader-buyer and data showing how many of them are out there.

In many cases, audience is covered naturally during the discussion of marketing and comps, and if you prefer to cover these items in a different order, the important thing is to cover this information, not how it's organized. In many cases, however, it is worth addressing the audience directly and with some researched numbers in a final two or three paragraphs.

Let's look at an imaginary example. Dr. Astra the astronomer wants to publish a general audience book in the category of maritime history and celestial navigation. She wants to write about the history of the Big Dipper and its role in shaping the world (or at least the world market) as we know it. A publisher will be able to extrapolate pretty quickly that there is a certain market for so-called big-science books, and Dr. Astra probably wants to mention that her title works in that category, especially when she's thinking about comparable titles.

But a publisher might not be aware that Dr. Astra's book (as she believes) is going to be of keen interest to the estimated three or four million yacht club members across America. Sailing by the stars, after all, is part of the legacy and lore of sailing. She would be wise to offer her agent and editor some data from a trade journal showing that there is a large audience waiting for this book (and already buying similar titles), that this is an audience growing at a rate of seven percent a year since 2018, and that the more than a thousand yacht clubs in the country when polled have reported that their number one wish-list priority is increasing their offerings of boating-related speaker content. That is market-specific information that a publisher might not know, and Dr. Astra is making a good business argument that her marketing plan is likely to be effective and that there is a preexisting readership that will find this title of interest. Dr. Astra, of course, will want to mention that she is a member of her local yacht club and already has interest in book-related events from three yacht clubs in her area.

What does this section of a book proposal look like? I'm going to take a cue from Dr. Astra. Here's a sample for our Mary Ann Patten proposal.

> Audience & Comps. There has not been a previous biography of Mary Ann Patten, despite strong unpublished archival materials, primarily in the California state library system, including numerous first-hand press interviews with Patten at the time. The only directly competing titles are a fictional novel inspired by her story (Kelly, *The Captain's Wife*, Plume, 2002) and a self-published history of the clipper ship (Simpson, *Neptune's Car*, 2017), which includes the Patten story in several chapters.
>
> The title will appeal to readers broadly interested in narrative nonfiction and American history, as well as readers interested in business history; timely stories about the Antarctic, with a historical focus; yachting and boating; women's biography; and extreme adventure.
>
> The extreme adventure market has proven a particular successful demographic, with comparable titles such as Preston's *Lost City of the Monkey God*, Lansing's *Endurance*, and Grann's *Lost City of Z*. This title capitalizes on the current news cycle as well. Antarctica is a topic of considerable news coverage due to the effects of climate change. According to a recent article in the *New York Times*, the tourism market to Antarctica has doubled in the past decade and is "edging toward the mainstream" (February 26, 2020), and this title will be an attractive entrant into that growing reader-traveler market. Narrating a thrilling, true-life Antarctic survival story, with a following-in-the-footsteps component, at a moment when climate change may be ushering in a blue-ocean event that would herald the end of the Antarctic as it has been known in history, the

Patten biography is well positioned to attract readers from across this demographic of readers.

The yachting market is estimated in the United States at more than three and a half million participants annually, and U.S. Sailing reports that this market has expanded substantially during the Covid pandemic, with new interest among educated and culturally interested consumers growing (www.ussailing.org/wp-content/uploads/2018/01/Demographics2010.pdf). As demographic reports note, outside speakers on yachting topics are in particularly high demand at the thousand-plus yacht clubs across the United States, providing strong marketing and promotional networks. Strong, historical comparable titles in the maritime section include such bestselling works such as Junger's *The Perfect Storm,* Larson's *Dead Wake,* or Greenlaw's *Hungry Ocean.* Recent comps in this sector include Cameron's *Blood in the Water* (Viking, 2021) and Sancton's *Madhouse at the End of the Earth* (Crown, 2022).

The market for stories of remarkable women remains robust, with historical comparable titles including Mazzeo's own bestselling *The Widow Clicquot;* recent comparative titles include Purnell's *A Woman of No Importance* (Penguin 2020) and Bren's *The Barbizan* (Simon & Schuster, 2022).

The proposed Patten biography also fits comfortably into the very broad demographic of readers interested in American history (comps: Ambrose, *Undaunted Courage;* Pearl, *Taking of Jemima Boone*), including stories of the Gold Rush (and the gold standard), global trade, pandemics, and westward expansion (comps: Wilkerson, *Warmth of Other Suns*). This book benefits from strong regional marketing tie-in both in the California market and in the Maine-Boston-New York City markets.

This title is intended to be positioned between the large American history and biography market and the large adventure market, drawing readers interested in both categories and on new archival research to tell a fresh story of a woman who defied stereotypes and overwhelming odds.

Is this prose style that is going to set the world on fire? Nope. Neither is it encyclopedic. But it did what it was intended to do: it went into a good book proposal that got us a good trade contract. My best advice for writing the book proposal is also to keep functionality in mind and not get too caught up in fussing either. Keep the writing clear and tidy, and then just get on with it.

Chapter 7

THE BOOK PROPOSAL

Marketing and Author Platform

An effective book proposal also needs a section on the author and on marketing. This is not marketing that the publisher will do. For that, there will be a professional in-house publicist and marketer, and they will manage the press side of promoting your book after it's acquired. The marketing section that an editor wants to hear about in the book proposal is what you, as an author, can bring to the table and how you will be hand selling your book through a complementary strategy that you have developed.

For many authors — academic or otherwise — their hearts sink at this news. Promoting ourselves, pitching ourselves, especially as new entrants in a market, can feel uncomfortable. This is also probably the one segment of the book proposal where it would be wise to do some preparation well in advance. If you are toying with the idea of trying to write trade nonfiction, this is the place to start while you are thinking about the options.

Author and marketing will be the next substantial section(s) of a book proposal, and when you are starting to think about a transition to writing for general audiences, there sometimes does need to be

---

some working backward toward what in publishing you'll hear described as your author platform.

Among the academic authors I work with, the author component is typically a source of some anxiety and often misconceptions, and the marketing component is generally new territory. I usually focus it in this way: marketing, author, and audience are the three sales components that allow a well-written big book to reach a big readership (read: have big sales). My rule of thumb for new entrants into trade publishing is that you want to nail two of those three things (author, audience, or marketing), and one of them must be audience. Keep in mind that audience does not mean an audience of readers. It means an audience of book buyers, and it's a stand-in for the book market. Your proposal needs to address all three components, but it's fine if either the author or the marketing sections are somewhat thinner than the rest.

What this means in practice is this: if you are a relatively unknown author, without what is known as a broad author platform, then you need to make sure the marketing section is very strong and creative. On the other hand, if you are an author with a large pre-built platform, it's probably all right to have a relatively straightforward marketing plan. Let's break down these sections in a bit more detail.

Author and author platform: everything about your proposal, from the narrative summary to the marketing section and your sample chapter, needs to convey the message that this is a general audience book capable of supporting significant projected sales. The author section of your book proposal answers the question: What can you, the author, bring to the table in helping the publisher reach and communicate with that book-buying audience about this book? That is your author platform.

Expertise is one important part of your platform. If you're writing the next new "Diet Your Way to Health" book, it matters whether you are a licensed nutritionist, a medical doctor, or a research scientist. You would at least want to have a strong track record as a science writer communicating fact-based research effectively to general audiences. If you are pitching a general audience book about medieval history, it certainly helps if you are a medieval historian. As an academic, you will have expertise. That expertise alone isn't enough to get a trade book contract, but it is a strong entry point. What you want to focus on is connecting that expertise with an ability to speak with authority (we're good at that in academics) and in an engaging way (we're sometimes not so good at that in academics) to general audiences (not an academic strength).

Again, keep in mind that your expertise does not necessarily have to be your academic research field and certainly not your academic research field right now. You want to be thinking of your training and potential professional expertise from a wide lens, and your personal interests are also fair game. I was trained in comparative literature and culture. My first bestselling title was based on my real-life expertise in drinking champagne. I brought to that book project all my experience in archival research and all my historical training, and there were certainly moments when my academic background came into things substantially. At the time, however, the role of women in the champagne industry was not my research specialization. Today, I am very much an expert in that field. I routinely give academic lectures (as well as non-academic lectures) on the history of women in the wine industry and have taught courses in business and management schools on the wine industry since the publication of *The Widow Clicquot,* despite the fact that my entrance into the world of wine and the wine business began as a trade writing project. For mid-career academics, especially, writing for general audiences is an opportunity to write about topics that interest you. If the topic doesn't interest you, after all, it is unlikely to interest ten thousand (or fifty thousand) readers.

In my experience, the more personally connected you are to the project and the more ways it intersects with who you are as a person and the things you are authentically passionate and knowledgeable about, the easier this is to make happen. And, when the writing is absolutely miserable — and it will be at some point, because that is writing — that authentic connection to the self makes getting over the hard parts a lot more manageable. I have learned more than I could have imagined writing for general audiences and have met some amazing and inspiring people along the way, but that has happened, I am entirely certain, only because my intellectual and personal interest in what I was writing about was central. If you can figure out the place where your academic life or training and your authentic self (or, indeed, selves) connect, that is your trade topic.

If expertise, including personal arenas of knowledge, are one part of the equation, the ability to connect with general audiences is the other part of an author platform. If you are just beginning and don't have a platform for communicating with general audiences, begin it. You don't need a vast résumé. You need a couple of things you can point to that show you're committed to the endeavor. Reach out to your local library and offer to host a three-part public series on something connected to whatever it is you want to be a public expert on. Reach out to your church, your club, the local museum. My recommendation is to think of this like the extracurriculars part of a college application and to volunteer for something. Think about how to reach a substantial group of general audience people and how to document that.

———

This often means stepping outside our comfort zones and asking for an opportunity. Without getting too saccharine about it, I am a big believer in the truth of a certain piece of advice by the German writer Johann Wolfgang von Goethe: "Whatever you can do or dream, begin it. Boldness has genius, power, and magic in it." There is something to be said for audacity.

Do you need to start tweeting and throw yourself into social media? Do you need to pitch the *New York Times* for a contentious op-ed? You don't. If you enjoy social media or if you enjoy writing op-eds, by all means go for it. But the skills required to do either of those things successfully are not the same skills required to write a bestselling trade nonfiction title, and the social media landscape, in particular, is quickly evolving. If you hate doing it, it will be obvious, too, and it's hard to do well something you find mind-numbing (or worse, makes you resentful). If you already have fifty thousand followers and enjoy the razzle-dazzle, that's one thing. If you don't already have a large social media presence, though, the evidence that joining Facebook or X or another platform will matter for your trade book sales is thin on the ground.

While legacy social media can be a tool to drive book sales in individual cases, publishers are increasingly recognizing that the relationship between an author's social media presence and actual book sales is unpredictable and that, while there may be a correlation, it's not clear there is causation. There was a good *New York Times* article on this by Elizabeth Harris, encouragingly titled for this social media refusenik, "Millions of Followers? For Book Sales, 'It's Unreliable,'" (February 7, 2021). I've been told by social media coordinators and publicists at Big Five houses as recently as 2023 that their advice to authors at this point is, if you don't already have a large social media platform, it's not necessary to try to develop those outlets. The algorithms that control the content users see on social media make the platforms less useful. Fake followers and bots are easy to purchase.

The social media that do seem to still have the ability to move book sales, circa 2023, are 2.0 platforms such as Bookstagram, BookTube, and BookTok (that is, book-specific Instagram, YouTube, and TikTok channels), but no one is certain for how long that will be effective. It tends to be a youth-oriented and rapidly shifting ecosystem. The algorithms on the internet, as well, are weighed to move the platform in the direction of paid content and advertising, and we're seeing a tendency for free social media to become less effective over time.

Keep in mind, too, that just as trade contracts are geared toward thousands or tens of thousands of books sold, likewise the kinds of numbers on social media that are likely to impress a potential trade publicist are larger. If you have fifty thousand followers, by all means you can leverage that and it likely will be a positive factor when the publisher is considering your proposal, but be aware that a few thousand academic friends and Mom following you on social media is not only not going to move the dial with a publisher but, if you try to make too much of it, may send the message that you aren't aware of the scale and reach hoped for by general audience marketing departments. In general, however, you can simply note any genuinely substantial social media or other networks in your section on the marketing plan. Otherwise, skip it.

If you are going to work to develop a social media presence as an author platform, because you do need to have something on your side of the balance sheet, just be sure your social media accounts and publications function as an amplifier for your general audience communications and aren't working at cross purposes. Remember, in

---

other words, that the goal is book sales. It is easy to confuse impact and sales, as I've mentioned earlier. The academy cares about impact. Trade publishers don't care about impact, unless impact drives sales. With polemical social media, that relationship is complicated. As we've already said, there is a lot of research showing that most of what gets shared on social media is emotional content, and the emotional content that is most likely to hook a reader is something infuriating. I question whether thirty thousand people who hate your post sharing it with other people they think will also hate it is building the kind of platform you are going to enjoy having—and whether those thirty thousand are likely to buy your book. I'm pretty careful, for example, not to share a whole lot about my personal politics because a substantial subset of my readers come to my work from other subcultures, and we live in a fairly polarized moment.

If you would like to write commentary for news outlets—national or local—or develop your own subscription-based newsletter on Substack, of course that is one route to building an author platform, and it certainly is one that in a book proposal publishers will recognize too. Different people choose different paths. The reality, as Elizabeth Harris notes, is that what actually does reliably drive book sales are reviews in major publications. If you have personal contacts in journalism, your publisher will certainly be delighted to hear that. Otherwise, this is beyond your control and something you can be assured your publicist will be working hard to secure, months before publication.

You don't have to start posting or starring daily on your own TikTok channel. You do have to do something. Potential publishers will also recognize community engagement, public speaking, and volunteer work as platform, so just be aware that there are other options. The other thing that does seem to drive book sales is personal connections, and those can be real rather than simply virtual. The way to start establishing personal connections with your readers is by presenting yourself as an author.

Presenting yourself as an author starts with a personal webpage. I strongly recommend, by way of an author platform, a personal website, not affiliated with your academic institution, although it is perfectly all right to provide a link to your academic biography. I recommend developing this while you are working on your book proposal and plan to have the webpage live by the time you send out the finished proposal, so an editor can look at it. Much of what is on the webpage will cross over with the content in your author section of the book proposal, and it can be a good adjunct to your book proposal once you populate it.

Your author website can be relatively simple. In its first iteration, all you need is a landing page with your biography, a photograph, and a gallery with a couple of general audience samples. Later, you will have a separate page for each book, plus highlighting of all your positive reviews and media successes. Your biography on the webpage can be the same paragraph or two that you use to introduce your author section in the book proposal.

You do not need to hire a professional designer to create your website, as long as you are reasonably technologically competent and keep your website relatively simple. There can be a temptation to add all sorts of bells and whistles, and that's fine if you can manage it reliably or if you have funds to hire a designer, but it isn't necessary if you keep things simple. If you know you are not technologically savvy enough to tackle even a basic webpage, many universities have professional development offices and work-study students who can help build one; it is worth asking around at your institution.

You do need, as well, a professional photograph — a "head shot" in trade lingo. Resist the temptation to use your favorite recent personal snapshot. Hire someone with lighting and knowledge of what they are doing. You need two photographs, one from the waist up, and one face and shoulders only, saved as high-resolution digital files in both color and black-and-white. Be sure you own the rights to the images and ask how the photographer wishes to be credited. Be sure you specify high resolution. You want something friendly but with a neutral facial expression. Post one on your website, and the others you can set aside for media requests when — let's be audacious here — you get them. You should expect to pay in the region of five hundred dollars for professional photos, give or take a hundred, unless you can persuade your academic institution to offer studio head shots for faculty as a benefit, which would be another worthy thing to harass a dean about, in my opinion.

Resist as well the temptation to talk about your academic monographs or publications on your personal website, unless they have general audience appeal. That work should be prominently displayed on your university-based webpage, and you should certainly link to that page in your biography. Just add a link to the part of your biography that lists your academic affiliation, and let a viewer navigate over to your institution to learn more about your research. The personal website, however, is for your trade-author persona, and everything about it should be public facing.

It can be hard to leave your academic accomplishments out, especially in the beginning, when you may not have much in the way of content to highlight. For academic writers making the first book pitch, it's those three to five general audience items that cause the most anguish. If you don't have content, you may want to take some time before you send out your first book proposal to develop material you can highlight here (though it's not strictly necessary).

If you decide to put together these general audience "clips" so you can showcase them to an agent or publisher as part of your book proposal, then the goal of this section is to show that you have some track record of communicating with broad audiences in an engaging manner and to show that you have a platform, however nascent, that you can bring to marketing your title. Giving a lecture to the local community center on your general audience topic? Get someone to record or video it. Not giving one? Volunteer. Have you written something for general audiences that appeared in a magazine or newspaper? Link to it. And if you don't have it, think about how to create it. Reach out to your local public or campus radio station and offer to give an interview or host a segment. Ask your university development and media office to help you record a video or other content; media offices on campus will generally work with you to develop high-quality content that they can also share with alumni, parents, and students. Remember how we all got our first publications by writing reviews or encyclopedia articles back in graduate school? You already know how to do this building a new c.v. thing. Just start at the beginning — and replace c.v. with author platform.

Before you can effectively write your author-platform section of a book proposal, then, you need to think about what you can bring to the table. You bring your expertise. And you want to bring some evidence to show that you can communicate to a general audience. This section is a combination of your biography and a personal pitch about why you are well positioned to reach a large number of interested book buyers.

Finally, you are going to need a well-crafted author biography. Here's my basic structure for this section of your book proposal: a short segment on author biography, which you reuse on your author webpage, focused on your expertise, your general audience credentials, and any "personal passion" connection to your proposed topic. Here's a (fictional) example of an author biography.

Dr. Johnny Appleseed is a nationally renowned expert in heritage fruit-tree propagation and the Famous Donor Chair of Fruit Sciences [hot link here to Dr. Appleseed's university webpage] at Land Grant University. Over a twenty-year career, he has traveled extensively across the United States speaking to public audiences on home-orchard preservation. His humorous and accessible plant-information sheets for Agricultural Extension have earned him a wide, if irreverent, following. Dr. Appleseed now combines his passion for "plain speaking" with his world-class reputation in horticulture to bring to general readers his trade nonfiction title *An Apple a Day: A Home Gardener's Guide to the Heritage Orchard*. Dr. Appleseed is one doctor no reader will want to keep away. A confirmed bachelor, Dr. Appleseed lives with his two golden retrievers, Adam and Eve, on Long Island.

On Dr. Appleseed's website, his aptly named endowed chair would link directly to his university affiliation, and there we can read all about his acres of published research. If I were this author, I'd probably post on this website a regular professional head shot and a second (also professional) photo of myself with two adorable puppies. Because, yes, everyone really does love puppies, including journalists looking to get eyeballs on their content. In his gallery, Dr. Appleseed could post three different general audience items: a PDF of an information sheet for Agricultural Extension, a video of himself giving an entertaining public lecture on home orchard preservation, and a local "at-home" newspaper article on his personal orchard, with members of the public visiting on tour at harvest.

One of the takeaways should be that those three general audience items are not impossible to generate. You can easily do what Dr. Appleseed did here. If you volunteer as a renowned professor to write some free content or give a public workshop, or if you invite your neighbors to come pick some of your heritage apples in the autumn and learn about cidermaking, someone is going to take you up on that offer. Local newspapers, tourist bureaus, and chambers of commerce, especially, are often looking for feel-good content. Remember, too, that local newspaper stories show up just as readily in an internet search for your name as material from the BBC World Service, if that's what's available.

Part of what you're also doing is assembling a network. At all of these occasions Dr. Appleseed is meeting people. The venues you can access and the people you know are important components of an author platform. What book publishers know is that it's the one-to-one connection that sells books to readers.

How can you grow your network of real connections to real people on a one-to-one basis? If Dr. Appleseed is smart, he'd make sure to find a way of gathering the email addresses of the people who enjoyed his information sheets and workshops. Maybe he offers copies of his Agricultural Extension archive on his webpage, sent by email, complimentary, to anyone who registers. Maybe he offers each springtime a free extra newsletter to anyone who sends him his email address. Maybe Dr. Appleseed opens his webpage to questions about gardening from readers and posts his answers there. Then, in the marketing section of his book proposal, Dr. Appleseed can boast that he has a subscriber database of ten thousand people, all of whom will be interested to hear about his forthcoming title.

One-to-one connections with readers don't necessarily require that you, as the author, connect individually with each person. It

---

simply requires that each person feels a personal connection to you as an author. You can make that connection by talking to three hundred people, but just be sure to make time to answer audience questions, make eye contact, and readily accept and offer business cards. Selling books is part sales and part entertainment. Be yourself, and be a little bit shameless.

Remember, the marketing section of your proposal does not need to explain what the publisher could or should do to sell your book. You don't need to detail for the publisher how, as part of the marketing plan, they should send a review copy of your book to the *New York Times*. You can certainly list niche general audience venues that a publisher might not otherwise be aware of, but in general this section is asking what, on top of their regular publicity and sales channels, you can do and who you can connect with in order to sell books.

What about book tours? Once upon a time, the book tour was how an author helped to sell and promote a title. Let go of this idea in your proposal. The book tour is another one of those older forms of marketing that no longer drive sales effectively. Especially post-Covid, getting a large audience turnout for book signings is increasingly challenging. Even when there is an audience, there are relatively few sales, on a dollar-for-dollar basis. Publishers often still contractually ask that you be available for a book tour, in case the title gets the kind of media traction where those make sense, but book tours are, in fact, relatively uncommon for nonfiction titles, unless you are a celebrity or your book is an exceptionally big title.

For many authors, the idea of the book tour is steeped in a certain romance and glamor. If you are struggling to let go of the idea, let me introduce you to the reality of the book tour. You will end up flying two thousand miles in economy class. You'll probably get stuck in a middle-row seat back by the toilets, because that's what flying today is. You're going to show up at a bookstore where there are six people in the audience. The guy in the front row will be nodding off while you're speaking. The man hovering nearby is still deciding whether to take a seat or not, because being in an audience of six feels like a commitment. The woman in the back row is the bookseller who organized the event. The three women in the middle (about sixty-five percent of books sold are purchased by women) all listen attentively, and you are grateful for the eye contact and nodding. The man ultimately wanders off during your reading. The three women come up afterward and tell you how much they loved your book talk and how they can't wait to check your book out of the library (read: no sales). The bookseller, smiling apologetically, asks you to sign a half dozen copies of your book, and at least you know you can count those as book sales. Once a book is signed, at least the bookseller can't return those copies to the publisher.

Open your proposal, hover your cursor, and delete that sentence about the book tour. Book tours and bookstore signings, unless you are well-known in the community and are bringing your own network to the event, are generally not effective at generating either publicity or sales. If your publisher wants you to do one, let them arrange it. What can be effective, however, is to think about ticketed events that you can help organize where a copy of your book might be included in the admission. I've had very good success with this approach and have often arranged to speak to large audiences of up to two hundred people at a time, with two hundred guaranteed book sales. From a publisher's perspective, events that an author undertakes to arrange with a certain guaranteed number of sales are precisely what they are looking for.

Curious to try this approach to author events? You want to begin by thinking about who the reader-buyer for your book is. If your book is positioned as a vacation read, ask a beachfront hotel if they are looking for a free, lively (and you will need to be lively) happy-hour speaker. If your book is on French history, reach out to the French cultural heritage center. If your book is on fish, get in touch with the aquarium. If your book is on local history, contact the tourism bureau. Identify who your (different) readers might be and think about where you can propose a special event—especially one where a copy of your book is included in the price of the ticket. Keep in mind that organizations, businesses, and people are predictably looking for material that bridges the gap between education and entertainment, especially around the winter holidays, summer holidays, and Mother's Day. Mother's Day, especially, is one of the highest demand days for add-in programming.

Dr. Appleseed, for example, might propose in the marketing section of his proposal to offer workshops at major botanical gardens and local cideries. Who doesn't want to go a cider tasting and learn more about apple seeds as part of the experience? What cidery doesn't want to host an event that will get more people through their doors drinking and buying their cider? Who doesn't want to take Mom out for a cider-tasting brunch on Mother's Day and know that the ticket includes a signed copy of a gardening book as a present for her? Botanical gardens want to draw visitors for admissions. Garden centers want to offer events for customers. Dr. Appleseed will donate his time—but the price for the event needs to include a signed copy of his new title. The publisher will generally offer special pricing, usually at a forty percent discount, to make that an appealing proposition for the hosts.

Dr. Appleseed might suggest in his book proposal setting up a half dozen of these events during the first six weeks of the book's launch. This period immediately following the publication of a book is considered crucial in the trade publishing industry. If Dr. Appleseed is feeling social media savvy, he would of course propose to chronicle his cross-country round-trip on his webpage or on social media. Realistically, he is going to be paying for the cost of this trip himself, as one of his author-related business expenses, so he is going to make sure he's also thinking of his road trip as an adventure. He would, however, ask his publicist to help him arrange local newspaper interviews at stops along his itinerary as the publisher's contribution, and it is not an insignificant contribution. A publisher generally budgets ten percent of an advance for marketing and publicity, and the single most important part of that budget is the expertise of a publicist.

Dr. Appleseed's publicist is going to be happy to try to set up those media interviews. It's a win-win situation. The publisher knows that Dr. Appleseed is going to put time, effort, and ingenuity into reaching his audience and that, if his marketing plan works, there will a couple of hundred guaranteed book sales — book sales that, happening in the crucial early weeks, will serve double duty as word-of-mouth promotion. Dr. Appleseed has also given his publicist some specific and realistic media targets on which they can cooperate. Extra points to Dr. Appleseed, too, if he can write in his book proposal that he has personal contacts at any of these proposed venues.

What if you're not Dr. Appleseed? What is your marketing plan if you're a professor of medieval history or astronomy or geology? It's the same principle, just different variables. You're looking for places where your expertise connects with your audience. Dr. Addie Astra the astronomer, with her book on constellations, can reach out to those yacht clubs and offer a stargazing course on celestial navigation. A copy of her new trade book, *The Out-of-This-World Origins of the Big Dipper,* will be included, of course, in the ticket. Clubs, orga-nizations, charitable galas, institutions, and businesses, especially businesses where your topic connects in some way to their core enterprise, are all good options because they have their own contact networks and can help publicize your event as part of their outreach. I know two people who got their first general audience experience by speaking to the local Rotary Club, where they found a very recep-tive audience.

A word, while we are on the topic of Dr. Astra's new book, about ti-tles. You are going to need a provisional title in your book proposal. It will be provisional. Titles and covers, under the terms of most trade contracts, are decisions ultimately made by the publisher and the sales team, not by the author. That is different from academics. As an author, you will certainly be asked for your input on the title, and you will be part of the process. You will certainly be given a say when it comes to the final selection of the cover design. Usually you'll be asked in the beginning if you have any images or ideas, and then asked at the end of the process for your preference between two or three final designs.

No one wants an author to be unhappy with either a title or a cover. However, the job of the marketing and sales teams is to mar-ket and sell your book, and titles and covers can matter hugely in how a book is seen and positioned in the market. So let them do their job. If you have a reasonable and strongly held objection, by all means speak up. Otherwise, your motto in trade publishing, as in life, should be: Don't be a pain in the ass.

Your goal at this stage of the book proposal is to come up with a provisional title that is catchy, shows you understand how titles po-sition a book in the market, and speaks to what is timely, relevant, and gripping about your project. Remember when you were coming up with an idea for a general audience book how you wanted to tick all those boxes? That's what you're repeating in your development of a title. Titles tend, in particular, to emphasize a character, story, something gently contrarian, or something timely — or all four. As I was writing this, I pulled up the current *New York Times* nonfiction bestseller list, and here are a few of the titles: *River of the Gods: Genius, Courage, and Betrayal in the Search for the Source of the Nile; Secret City: The Hidden History of Gay Washington; The Man Who Broke Capitalism: How Jack Welch Gutted the Heartland and Crushed the Soul of Corporate America — and How to Undo His Legacy.*

The format is, in essence, a short lead title (which can be printed in big bold letters on the cover), a colon, followed by a subtitle that hints at some narrative, new discovery, new solution, or mystery. If I were coming up with a provisional title for a book proposal, I would (and do) use that basic formula.

In the book proposal, your marketing activities section should run a couple of paragraphs, and in general I would recommend coming up with three different ways in which you can leverage your author platform to support book sales. Dr. Appleseed, for example, is going to propose his cross-country botanical event series and is going to be sure to mention his book in his upcoming newsletter on his author webpage and in his biography on all his new Agricultural Extension information sheets. Dr. Appleseed still needs to demonstrate in his book proposal, however, that there are book buyers who are going to be interested in his title. There's no point in coming up with plans to reach an audience that doesn't exist. He needs to show not only that he has some good marketing ideas and that his book is marketable, but that there is a market.

Chapter 8

THE SAMPLE CHAPTER AND
THE BUSINESS OF WRITING

The last section of your book proposal is the place where you show an agent and editor that you have the communication skills to write on this proposed topic for a general audience — and, indeed, that you have the skills to write a bestseller, if that's your aspiration. This, the sample chapter, is arguably the most important section of a book proposal. The only other contender is the narrative summary, to which the sample chapter is closely linked. The sample chapter is critical because it shows an editor one of two things: you are either writing engaging narrative for a trade audience — or you are not.

This is also not something that anyone can show you how to do in a precise way. There is no way to give you a "sample" sample chapter that can keep open all the options you want to keep open when you're thinking about how to approach this. How you write your sample chapter depends on a whole range of particular circumstances about your material, your idea, your audience, and your narrative that just can't be generalized or imitated. So let's focus instead on a toolkit of skills that trade writers deploy — and that you may wish to use when you are writing your sample chapter. That toolkit is going to be the focus of the final chapters.

For the moment, let's look at the work the sample chapter needs to perform in a book proposal in a general way and then consider what to do with a book proposal once it's complete. The book proposal, after all, is only a means to an end, and the end is a trade book contract. It's important to understand that a sample chapter is not really a sample chapter. In other words, it is not a chapter that is ever actually going to exist in the final book. That's not only because the shape of any book, contracted on the basis of a proposal only, is going to evolve in the writing process and in dialogue with an editor, but because it is not actually meant to function as a real chapter. What the sample is showcasing is not an actual section of a provisional book; it is demonstrating your ability to write for a general audience in a compelling way—using your proposed topic as the occasion—and showcasing your proposed topic as a general audience topic.

Because one of the two functions is to pitch your topic as a trade title, your sample chapter does need to come from the book you are proposing. You would not want to give a writing sample from a different project and especially not from an academic project. The sample chapter carries a great deal of weight. It is worth working on carefully and revising. An agent can help you finesse a marketing and audience section. An editor can help you tweak chapter outlines as long as your book proposal has some good bones to the structure. The narrative summary and the sample chapter, though, are fundamental: you have a great general audience book idea and have to be able to show that you can write engagingly for general audiences. If you don't have those two things, you're not going to make it to the next stage of the conversation.

———

How to plan, then, a sample chapter? The first question is what moment in your proposed book to highlight and make the central arc of your writing sample. What you want to do, strategically, is to think about one particularly dramatic, interesting, or important moment in your proposed book. This moment is probably not the opening chapter, in particular. Writing beginnings is notoriously tricky.

Generally, I find that narrating the false pivot is an easy place to focus. As you'll remember from our earlier discussion of the false pivot, this is the point in your project where it looks like something is going to move in one direction but ends up going in another. It can be the moment where the data appears to be heading toward one conclusion — and then something appears that changes the entire picture. It can be the moment we expect one thing but get another. In a general way, you're looking for something that creates a kind of natural cliffhanger.

Once you have decided on a section of your proposed book to use as a sample chapter, spend some time thinking about how you want to structure that chapter, keeping in mind that a sample chapter does not need to be a full four thousand words. I generally write sample chapters that are about half that length. What matters is that your sample chapter shows that you understand how to write a trade book and how to work with tightening and loosening narrative tension.

What is crucial to recognize is that not only books have narrative arcs, so do individual chapters. You do need something propulsive that carries your reader over the gap from one chapter to the next. Think about the experience of your general audience reader: that person on the flight from Seattle to Boston who has picked up your book in the airport; that commuter on the subway from the Bronx to

Manhattan; that soccer mom or dad, sitting in the SUV somewhere in Kansas waiting for a game to wind up in the next twenty minutes. That person has a whole series of claims on his or her attention and is looking for a book with a structural framework that gives a reader multiple points of entry and exit.

If I am that soccer mom, and I put this book down in the back seat of the car on Monday, can I pick it back up on Wednesday and get back into the flow? Did the writer leave me enough structural points of engagement? If I can't get back into the story, that book is likely to end up on Friday in the trunk, alongside the kids' wet shoes and water bottles. This is one of the reasons why chapters in general audience books tend to be shorter than in academic titles: the average chapter is something the average person can read in under fifteen minutes.

The function of the narrative arc in general audience chapters is to make each chapter satisfying to read as a unit, and, in order to create those entry and exit points, compelling chapters are also going to make it easy to pick the narrative back up and hard to put the book down. Functionally, this means you are trying to do three things: structure a chapter with a narrative arc, open the chapter by reminding the reader of what happened in the preceding chapter, and — here's the hardest part — end the chapter with something that is both a satisfying resolution to this chapter and looks ahead to the next chapter's tension, creating momentum.

In the sample chapter, a cliffhanger at the end is an easy way to accomplish this functionally, and I'd probably recommend using this as a kind of shorthand in your sample chapter to show that you understand how to work with dramatic tension in general audience writing. Over the course of a whole book, ending each chapter with a cliffhanger is going to look pretty formulaic and ham-fisted, so you'll ultimately want to find different and subtler ways of managing pacing. But that's all down the road, once you have the book contract, and we'll come back to this in later chapters.

For the moment, just take away from this that you need a sample chapter that highlights the timeliness and relevance of your topic and something that lends itself to narrative arc. Because the sample chapter is not a real chapter, you're looking for a scenario — one that in your final manuscript might span two or three chapters — where you can narrate the conflict, complication, and resolution that seem to you to define your project. If you need to use something that "belongs" in another chapter to make the sample chapter work, use it. You are not writing a real chapter-in-the-world; you are just showing what you can do with the material. And resist the urge to over-research.

Writing the manuscript will require expertise — in fact, multiple areas of expertise. Writing a book proposal does not require exhaustive research into the content of your project. The good news is that, as academics, we have spent our lives learning the two things that matter: we know how to conduct research and we know how to make ourselves expert in a field even if we are new entrants. The bad news is that, as academics, we can struggle with over-researching, both at the stage of writing the book proposal and later, at the stage of writing and completing the manuscript.

Quite simply, research is easier and more enjoyable than writing. I have seen academics who are unable to complete their manuscript (or unable to keep to word limits) because they aren't able to stop researching at some point and start writing and editing. We also can fall prey to the idea that, unless we are an expert, we can't speak on something competently. I invite you, therefore, as an academic to think of the book proposal and the sample chapter as proposals for research and writing and not as a research-based output. Apart from your agent and your publisher, no one else will ever see your proposal or sample chapter. You want to do enough research to write the proposal and book chapter well. Anything else at this stage is over-researching. Do the research you need to write the sample chapter. However, as we will discuss when we get to the practical writing part of this book, the research you need also may not be the research you think. For the moment, you want to have in mind what moment in your proposed work you can turn into a sample chapter of two or three thousand words.

You are going to need to cover a few other details, as well, in this book proposal, and one of the most important among them is the date you are going to deliver your manuscript. Deadlines—known as delivery dates in the trade—are also relatively circumscribed by certain market conditions, and this is a date you want to think about strategically. This is not a date to take lightly.

Let's again take a step back and think about how trade-book contracts work and how they are different from academic book contracts. We are talking here about academic publishers publishing on the academic and non-profit side of their lists, because academic presses can also have, of course, trade divisions. Academic publishers on the academic list side of things don't generally offer advance contracts, and they don't generally offer advances either on scholarly monographs. And that makes sense: when an academic publisher offers a contract for a scholarly monograph, the expectation is that the author has submitted the manuscript in advance, that manuscript has been read and reviewed by a certain number of anonymous external reviewers, and based on those peer reviews being positive, the press commits to publish the book. By the time the

book has been accepted contractually, it is ready to move into production. Occasionally, if someone has a tight tenure clock and the
complete manuscript has been submitted and there is one positive
review and a second reader is dawdling, a university press will write
a pre-contract letter. But in general, for scholarly monographs, delivery and acceptance are simultaneous with the book contract, and
although there are the same kinds of standard royalty terms in most
of those contracts, advances are unusual for titles where the sales are
unlikely to cover the costs of production. As you already know as an
academic, there is a running joke about fourteen-cent royalty checks
for academic authors.

What this means is that, if you've had a conversation with an
interested editor at an academic conference or over email, in which
he or she expresses interest in your scholarly monograph, and you
cheerfully promise to deliver the manuscript at the end of the summer, the university press editor doesn't really mind if that book arrives as promised or not. It doesn't cost the academic press anything
if your manuscript arrives six months or six years later. It will still
go out for peer review — to reviewers who are generally "paid" with
a few books from the warehouse, if at all — and it will either still be
current in the field or not.

If you accept a hundred thousand dollar advance from a Big Five
trade publisher, on the other hand, and you commit in a book contract to deliver that title at the end of the summer, the publisher is
going to be upset if you don't deliver the manuscript on time or give
plenty of early notice if you're going to deliver it late. If a publisher
offers you that kind of advance, that means a publisher is expecting
to sell sixty thousand copies or more and is trying to manage an initial print run of anywhere from five thousand (pretty modest) to
twenty thousand (nice) or more copies. They have scheduled some-

one on their team to copy edit that book, to market that book, to sell that book. A trade book contract, especially at a Big Five press, is a commercial business deal, and contractual deadlines in the trade publishing world are not suggestions.

It's not that people don't get delivery extensions on trade-book contracts. They do all the time. Life happens. Sometimes research takes an author in other directions. Even Big Five trade publishers can usually be flexible, as long as you give your editor generous advance notice and there is not something that makes the relevance of your title particularly time sensitive. Often, however, there is a clause written into trade contracts stipulating that if you deliver later than a certain window, the publisher can cancel the deal — and ask for a return of advances.

Keep in mind, as well, that the term is "delivery and acceptance" in trade book contracts for a reason. The delivery date that you are proposing is not the date of a first draft. It is the date by which you will deliver a publishable manuscript. Generally, after delivery, there will be a short period of final back-and-forth with an editor, maybe a few weeks, where the author may be asked to make some fine tuning before the book is officially accepted and goes to copy editing. However, by the time you get to the delivery date, your manuscript should require only what is known as line editing and not the heavier lifting known as developmental editing. That means, basically, you should be at the point of having to work out localized problems with a discrete and limited number of sections in the manuscript. At D&A you should not be still working out how to structure a narrative arc or looking to fill in research later.

My sincere advice, before you shoot off that book proposal, is to make sure you have blocked off the time you need to write this manuscript so you can deliver it on time before you commit to a particular delivery and acceptance date in a trade book contract. If you're an academic writing your first book on an advance contract, with just a book proposal, I strongly recommend thinking strategically about timing that to coincide with a period of otherwise light commitments.

I once wrote a trade book with a one-year contract-to-delivery deadline while acting as a chair of department, and even as someone quite experienced in the process at that time, I cannot recommend that strategy. Another time, I got a book contract with a short deadline and had to ask a dean for a year of unpaid leave on short notice. Although my dean was sympathetic and supportive and gave me the leave, I cannot honestly say that I made extra friends in my department when news broke that the curriculum had to be reorganized and someone else had to take my freshman composition section at the last minute. For my first trade book, things also happened more quickly than I would have anticipated: I sent off that proposal to an agent and in less than six weeks had not only an agent but also a book contract and a deadline for which I wasn't fully prepared. Proposal to book deal in six weeks is not the norm. But prepare for success.

I would also build in a grace period. Books take longer to write than we think, especially if you are writing a general audience book for the first time and are learning as you go. If you happen to get a champagne lunch, you will be glad you gave yourself the time to rewrite that first third of the manuscript. I personally budget eight months to write a book, and ten months is a reasonable period for the research portion. But I am probably on the more rigid and self-disciplined side of the author spectrum, and I have more than a half dozen titles under my belt, so I tend to need to do less rewriting now than when I was starting. When I am writing, I also have a hard and fast rule: I write five hundred publishable words a day, six days a week, early in the morning. Some days, I make my goal by nine in the morning. Those are good days. Other days, I am still pulling my hair out at noontime. My experience, however, is that three or four hours a day and five hundred publishable words are achievable goals, even if you are teaching during part of the writing process. It is, of course, ideal if you can plan to not be teaching for any part of that period.

Keep in mind, as well, that because timeliness and relevance are generally factors and because these titles are more exposed to saturation and trends, delivery deadlines for trade titles, especially at a Big Five publishing house, tend to be shorter than might be acceptable for a scholarly monograph. It is not uncommon to work on an academic book for a decade or more, especially post-tenure. Occasionally trade books may take that long to deliver, but that is very much the exception if you are working on an advance contract. Delivery in eighteen to twenty-four months after signing the contract is about the norm for the Big Five. A lot longer than twenty-four or maybe thirty months and publishers — who have guaranteed you an advance on royalties — start to worry about whether the market will shift for your title and their sales calculations won't remain current. Shorter than eighteen months is tough for an author to handle. I have written a book on a twelve-month contract-to-delivery deadline, and someone would have to offer me a very large advance indeed to consider repeating that experience.

My recommendation, if you're thinking about pitching your first general audience title, is to propose twenty-four months for delivery, and try to give yourself either a free semester or a summer immediately preceding delivery. Once you're more comfortable with the process, eighteen months is a good delivery period, and don't be surprised if you're asked to trim delivery to eighteen months even on a first trade contract. I've often proposed the first of October as a delivery deadline, hoping to give myself a full summer to write, plus the first three weeks of the term, when things aren't usually too out of control and I could usually carve out some time if needed, at least to do something like proofread and finish up notes and a bibliography. Even better would be a fall term off, either on a planned sabbatical, fellowship leave, or unpaid leave (if the advance supported that), with a December 1 delivery date. This allows as much as six months for full-time writing, right at the end of the project, when I inevitably need it more.

You can propose whatever date you like, of course; everyone's academic schedule and family obligations are different. Just be aware that there is generally a year or more of lead time from delivery to publication. And be aware that there are generally three seasons in publishing, the fall, winter, and spring/summer lists. Because publishers acquiring a book are slotting it into a seasonal list, alongside a complement of other titles, as part of their consideration you might get a request to adjust the delivery deadline.

I cannot emphasize enough the importance of being professional about the business of writing. Unless you are certain that you only want to write one trade book, you want to think about your reputation with agents and publishers, especially if you are publishing with one of the Big Five, where academic pressures are going to be viewed with less understanding. Until certain tax-law changes in the United States in the 1970s and 1980s, there was a robust "mid-list" in trade publishing. These included authors whose books, over the course of a career, were profitable but not immediate bestsellers. Some books might do particularly well; other books, less well. But on average, these writers could continue writing and getting contracts. That meant, in effect, the second chances were more economically viable.

The trade market today is a narrower space, and in my experience reputation does matter, and second chances especially depend a great deal on it, at least among Big Five publishers. If you want to write a second or third trade book and be given a second or third contract if every title isn't a bestseller, you want to be known as someone who is professional and easy to work with. There is no guarantee of your next contract in trade publishing. Having tepid book sales and being a pain in the ass, however, is definitely not a winning combination.

My first trade book was a *New York Times* bestseller. My second book was not. My third book, as a result, was touch and go. I had an editor for that book who inherited me and my project mid-stream and who, based on my most recent BookScan numbers, wasn't enthusiastic about our prospects. My second book hadn't "earned out" — in other words, the press was losing money, not just on the book but also on the advance, and not earning out is frankly a deeply unenviable position to be in as a trade writer. In the years that followed, I have on occasion been willing to take a lower advance for a book that I felt deeply about but which represented a gamble for the press, simply to make sure I am going to be on the right side of that balance sheet. A book that earns out is a success. Modest successes are still wins. Losses are still losses.

That third book eventually went on to become a bestseller on the *New York Times* travel list and to hit the bestseller list for an extended period with the *Los Angeles Times,* but not immediately on publication, and that meant that for my fourth book I had to start all over again at the bottom rung. My fourth book was a very strong topic, and I worked a long time on making sure the book proposal was stellar. Part of the reason I was able to get a contract for it and overcome a second book with disappointing BookScan numbers, though, was because I delivered good, publishable work on time, and I didn't take criticism (even not very diplomatic criticism) personally (at least not in front of anyone but my partner).

Being a professional, in this context, means basically three things: you meet your contractual obligations (or negotiate changes in advance), you respect the boundaries between what an author controls and what marketing and the publishing house get to decide, and you separate your personal emotions from your professional communications. In fact, it's not a lot different from being a chair of a department.

I think it's also worth saying that the decision, as an academic, to publish with a Big Five publisher has some advantages and some disadvantages. There are two upsides to publishing with a Big Five press: the advances and the audience. Because the number of projected sales required to be considered by Big Five editors is higher, the advances are proportionally just larger. They are generally enough that one can begin to imagine affording an unpaid leave, and they are often generous enough to live on in a modest way. There is also greater publicity, and that does open up certain cultural opportunities that are undeniably exciting. Those opportunities open up certain different career trajectories.

Despite the larger advances, though, I don't want to sugarcoat it. It is tough to make a living as a trade author, because it tends to be feast or famine even with the big publishing houses. Contracts are generally spread out over two or three years. There is the agent's cut, if you're working with an agent (and with Big Five publishers an agent is not optional). There are self-employment taxes. As soon as you make the decision to start working on a book proposal for a trade contract, the first person to call is your tax accountant, because if you are going to pay self-employment taxes you darned well want to be taking deductions for business expenses.

However, making a living as a trade author, if you're good at it, is not impossible. I resigned from a tenured position after my sixth trade book, and I did that because the economic reality made it reasonable to do so. My income as a writer does not entirely replace my academic salary. However, as part of a two-person academic couple with a spouse and a house on another coast (and across a border), my income as a writer more than replaced my salary once we were able to cut out the costs of commuting and maintaining two households. Writing for trade with the Big Five and an agent is a viable alternative to an academic career, and that is especially true for underpaid contingent faculty and for faculty facing long commuting distances. It is a viable option as well if after mid-career you are looking for a graceful exit. And, as a one-off, especially immediately post-tenure, a trade book contract can ramp up an academic career, open a lot of new doors, and give you a handy nest egg.

That said, publishing consistently with a Big Five publisher is ultimately difficult to reconcile with a full-time academic appointment, unless you happen to be at a research-focused institution, in a large department, where leaves of absence are not going to be an issue. They are two different careers that don't synchronize over the long term easily. Early in my career, I had supportive and forward-looking senior administrators. Administrative staff changes, however, and different deans and provosts can have starkly different levels of commitment to public-facing scholarship, shall we just say. You may also find that, several trade books in, your c.v. no longer matches the kind of research profile that most search committees are looking for in candidates for lines that tend to be still quite narrowly defined and discipline specific.

If you think you may want to make a post-tenure move, for whatever reason, my advice is to do it before you go too far down the road of trade publishing. One trade book probably opens up some career opportunities, as long as that book is field adjacent, especially if it's on the trade list of a university press. If you want to write several trade books and grow an author platform as a public intellectual, and especially if you want to transition into Big Five contracts, make that last senior academic job move first, and then have at it, for as long as they will let you. Even post-tenure an unsupportive senior administrator can make things very difficult for you.

If you are on the tenure track but as yet untenured and if tenure is something you hope to obtain, I know this is not fashionable advice these days, but I would strongly recommend against writing a trade book pre-tenure unless it has a clear prestige value. Even then I would think long and hard about it. You want to play tenure safe, because it is such a high-risk proposition. That means, from my perspective, any pre-tenure trade book should only be a second, "bonus" book, following on an excellent academic monograph. It should probably have some grant funding attached to it, something like an NEH or a Mellon, something to show that it met a competitive threshold. And you want to talk with your chair and dean before submitting that book proposal, to understand if your institution will support this direction. Some institutions do not. Remember that senior administrators can change, and with them your prospects. Once you have tenure, well, the risks are substantially fewer.

Chapter 9

HOW NOT TO WRITE LIKE AN ACADEMIC

Character as Narrative Device

How do you begin writing your sample chapter? This is where you have to do the actual getting down to it of writing — and not writing "like an academic" but writing the kind of effective narrative that has the potential to reach broad audiences and impact them. It's the writing you'll eventually need, as well, in your book manuscript.

Much of what comes next is craft. What I mean is that narrative writing is so relentlessly specific to the particular story you are trying to tell and the particular problem you are trying to solve as a writer that there is no paint-by-numbers solution. However, in general, there are two places where you can begin working with some specific techniques and where the effect is very substantial — character development and sentence-level control of tension, especially in the transition between chapters. Once you see the difference, you will quickly find other ways to deepen that practice, either through watching what other writers do (and I strongly encourage reading other nonfiction writers when you are stuck, to see if you can learn different strategies that might help you) or by muddling through successive drafts until you find the organic solution.

—

I've said that narrative is, in effect, conflict-complication-resolution (story) plus character. Something (story) happens to someone (character). We spent the previous chapter looking at the story side of narrative, as a structural element. Characterization takes place at the sentence level.

What makes a "strong" character? Well, for one thing such a character is multifaceted and complex, and as a general rule you need in your writing to develop at least one character with whom the audience can identify. You'll remember that from middle-school English class as the protagonist. For the neuropsychologists, it's this identification with a character that releases the reader's feel good (and do good) hormones of effective narrative. For screenwriters, they talk about Blake Snyder's famous "Save the Cat" beat of story: the moment when the protagonist becomes a character who is real enough and interesting enough to us as readers to be worth rooting for.

We identify in particular with characters who are conflicted. They have desires, and they experience obstacles — some of which are internal and some external — that prevent them from obtaining those desires. They also have desires that are multiple and that are also not always aligned with each other. In short, they are human.

The strongest characters are the ones who are most richly challenged and who have internal and external motivations and obstacles, which in the time of story become a knot, parallel to plot, that the character must untangle before there can be resolution. I once wrote about Edda Ciano Mussolini, Benito Mussolini's daughter. Her husband was a cheat and a fool. But she loved him. Her husband was part of a coup against fascism and her father. Edda also loved her father and wanted to please him. Her father hated to disappoint Edda, but Hitler wanted Mussolini to show his loyalty by executing her husband. Mussolini was afraid of angering Hitler and also of losing his daughter. In the end, her husband is executed, and Edda, betrayed, vows to destroy her father. All a true story. None of them are nice people, but as characters they have the kind of character complexity usually reserved for Renaissance drama.

What you are looking to uncover in your research material when it comes to characterization are places where a character is crossed by a conflict between desire and reality and between competing motivations and desires. In practice, the external motivations and conflicts are usually obvious, and this means that what you are looking to understand to deepen your narrative is the internal component to what makes your character propulsive. Keep in mind that if you are using author-as-character in your narrative, you need to develop yourself as a character.

It is possible, in theory, to write a narrative in which there is only one character, I suppose, but in practice that is not how effective narratives generally develop. In practice, you also are looking for, at the very least, an antagonist. The antagonist doesn't need to be an evil character or a bad guy, although that is not uncommon. The antagonist needs to be blocking the protagonist from reaching a goal. Very often, there is also an effective third character in a narrative, which allows the writer to split off the protagonist's external conflict (antagonist) and internal conflict (third character).

How fully developed your protagonist will be depends, in part, on how central a role character plays in your narrative structure. Characters can have somewhat different roles in different kinds of stories, of course. A narrative can be either character-centered or plot-centered, or it can balance both.

Character-based narratives tend to rely more heavily on fully developed interior and exterior character motivations and conflicts, while plot-based narratives can sometimes get away with characters whose motivations and conflicts are primarily external. We tend in fiction to think of character-centered structures as literary and plot-driven narratives as popular. In nonfiction, that hierarchy isn't nearly so rigid. We find both character-centered and plot-centered structures that are equally effective and successful. It is important to remember that plot-centered does not mean there is no character — only that the narrative (external) shapes the character's trajectory more substantially than does the character's internal conflict. Character-centered does not mean, either, that there is no narrative — only that the character is shaping more substantially the narrative's trajectory.

Character is not the labor of the middle distance. It functions typically, at the first introduction, by toggling between the big picture of type (what kind of person is this) and salient detail (what detail represents this person as an individual and not a type). I go to my bookshelf and pull out a narrative nonfiction title. It is Linda Colley's *The Gun, the Ship, and the Pen* (Liveright, 2021). I turn to the first page:

> It was in Istanbul that Kang Youwei witnessed the transformation at work. Sixty years old, a philosopher and a reformer, he had been exiled from his native China on account of his politics, and was persistently on the move. . . . Kang Youwei arrived in Istanbul on 27 July, the day these army rebels succeeded in getting the constitution formally restored. Pushing his way through the crowds, cut off by language, but not from the excitement, he watched as 'Half-moon flags hung, people drink, hit drums, sung songs together and danced. People were chanting long live, it did not stop day and night, streets, parks and everywhere were the same . . . it is astonishing.'

Kang Youwei is a type: "sixty years old, a philosopher and a re-former." He has a conflict: he has been exiled and finds himself root-less. He is an individual, presented to the reader first though his own unique words and perception. Once again, we have the first hint, too, of a conflict and dramatic tension: what was the transformation that Kang Youwei witnessed? Read on to find out.

I put the book back and pull out the title next to it, Andrea Pitzer's *Icebound: Shipwrecked at the End of the World* (Scribner, 2021). I look to see: how does Pitzer introduce her character? She writes in the opening paragraphs of the book:

> In 1594, while Spain laid siege to the Netherlands in the third decade of a bloody war, Dutch navigator William Barents prepared to sail off the edge of the known world. . . . The historical record on William Barents before this moment is nearly a blank. Born in the northern Netherlands near the mid-point of the sixteenth cen-tury, he was likely in his forties when he left home on his first Arctic voyage, but the year of his birth is unknown. He had trained as a steersman and had a childhood fascination with maps that endured into middle age. 'I always had the inclination, from my youth on-ward,' he wrote of himself, 'to use all my qualities to portray in maps the islands that I roamed and sailed with all the surrounding seas and waters.' His most famous portrait shows a receding hair-line, dark hair, sloping shoulders, and a nose like a chisel. . . . As he stood on the docks about to begin his long, painful trek into im-mortality, he was so far from fame that history would not even re-cord the name of his boat.

William Barents is a type: "Dutch navigator." He is also individu-ated: he had a childhood fascination with maps; we hear his own voice; we see his portrait. And, yet again, that first hint of conflict and dramatic tension: the world is at war, Barents will sail off the edge of the known world, he—we stand with him in this moment on the dock—is not famous. Not yet. But read on. He will be. He will be. Whether he can survive to see that day is his conflict.

One way to select detail for characterization of a research subject is to ask yourself what seems incongruous: What is it about this person that surprises me, that I would not have expected? The gruff fisherman whose diary entries are lyrical and show an appreciation of poetry. The staid Professor Jones, our researcher-as-character, who ends up wearing out in the field a leather jacket and carrying a bullwhip and shoots vodka while answering to the nickname Indy.

If you're looking to start sketching out character and pulling that information out of your research, start by making a list of each main (that is, fully developed) character (including, if you are using this device, author-as-character) in your project. For each character, you want to be able to write down what they want and what stands in their way. You want each character to have an internal conflict and an external conflict. You want something internal standing in their way and something external. Where you have characters whose motivations or conflicts overlap with each other, those are the characters you need to place front and center in your narrative, because they are the characters able to do the work of loosening and tightening narrative tension and propelling story.

From there, how do we help the reader identify with these characters? How do we give them voice and a subjectivity that the reader can enter into? Let's consider two examples of general audience nonfiction written by academics who have successfully made the transition to trade and that are character-focused. The same techniques that are successful in character-focused narratives can be used in developing character in a narrative-focused structure. Character-focused structure is a technique that, in nonfiction, benefits hugely from the availability of memoir, letters, diaries, or other first-person material, although it can be done through less direct historical reportage, as we will see in a moment. The key point is that, as you are researching for a general audience nonfiction project, it is a very good idea to be looking for first-person materials, because they are extremely useful for the writing process.

Both Laurel Thatcher Ulrich's Pulitzer Prize–winning history, *A Midwife's Tale* (Vintage, 1991), and Jill Lepore's *Book of Ages* (Vintage, 2014), a history of Benjamin Franklin's sister and a National Book Award finalist, are essentially character-defined narratives. It's worth looking at both titles for a moment, because they illustrate two very different approaches to creating character voice and interiority using third-person (he/she/they) narrative. First, a look at the techniques.

Unless you were trained as an English professor, "free indirect discourse" is probably not a familiar term, but it is worth understanding because it is very useful in narrative nonfiction writing, even if you are writing a primarily plot-defined narrative. Direct discourse is speech (internal or external) that is directly attributed to the character by the author and involves direct speech (that is, a quotation): "The water is cold," Mary said (or Mary thought). Indirect discourse is when the discourse is attributed to the speaker or thinker by the author, but only indirectly (not in quotes): Mary said that the water was cold.

Free indirect discourse is discourse that is indirect (not in quotes) and is not attributed to the speaker or thinker by the author. The reader makes the attribution. The reader could attribute the discourse to the character, or the reader could attribute the discourse to the author. It is the disjunction between these two possible attributions that famously creates the wit of Jane Austen. So, for example,

—

"Mary watched the boys playing by the stream. Someone should have lectured them. The water was cold. The water was always cold this time of the year." What the reader does not know — but is tasked with deciding — is whether "The water was cold" is Mary's internal dialogue, the lecture she might wish to give the children, or whether "The water was cold" is the historian's statement of fact.

The ability of a character to sound like a historian is not particularly interesting. The ability of a historian to sound like the internal thought of a character, on the other hand, is extremely useful in developing character and using character to tighten or loosen narrative tension.

Free indirect discourse can be further intensified by using what in the narrative-theory trade we would call representative perception. Here, when you have discourse that might be attributed to the character, you can further develop character by using word choice that represents the character you are working to convey. The word choice is selected in order, effectively, to represent or to stand in for the (inferred) perception of the character. "The water was cold" is not highly inflected. "The water was exceedingly frigid" or "The water was butt-assed cold," however, are words attributable to two very different kinds of speakers.

The narrative nonfiction contract, again, does not admit of compromise. You cannot as a fact-based writer invent anything. You cannot directly or indirectly attribute words to Mary that you do not have a source documenting that Mary said or thought them. You cannot say the river was cold unless you know that it was February and unless you know from the (thankfully voluminous) historical weather records what the daily temperature was on the day you are describing that river.

However, you are perfectly at liberty as a nonfiction writer to use free indirect discourse. If the reader attributes the discourse to character rather than author, there is nothing underhanded in writing well and using language complexly. If you know that water was cold, you can write that the water was cold. If you prefer to describe the water as "butt-assed cold" rather than "exceedingly frigid," and you are not directly attributing that speech without a source, your choice of words is always in your control as a writer.

Let's look at how Jill Lepore manages character. She works skillfully with both free indirect discourse and representative perception in *Book of Ages*. She tends, in particular, to slide from historical statement with no discursive aspect to historical statement as free indirect discourse, often using a colon to set off the free indirect speech. She writes, for example,

> In England, titles and wealth went to the eldest son: he, alone, was entitled. A franklin had no title; he had only his freedom but, still, the eldest son could expect to inherit the estate: he was entitled, at least, to that. Younger sons scrambled. And therein, Franklin thought, lay true nobility. As Poor Richard put it, *Many a Man would have been worse, if his Estate had been better.* (10)

It's well managed. The first sentence offers readers a historical fact, followed by what the reader is inclined to read as a historian's clarification. The second sentence, however, slides toward representational perception with the discursive speech interrupters "but, still." Those interrupters, narratively, create the impression that we have moved from something written to something spoken. We say "um" in speech. We (usually) edit those stance adverbs out of our writing. When they are used, it creates the effect of spontaneous thought or speech, something akin to stream of consciousness.

The effect in this case, for Lepore, is that, by the end of the second sentence, the reader begins to wonder whether "he, alone, was entitled" is the thought of Franklin or a historical statement. It remains unattributed but ambiguous. It can, of course, be either, which is precisely the point of free indirect discourse. The third sentence: "Younger sons scrambled." Once again, it is a thought free of attribution, and, if the reader had any doubts about whether it might be discourse attributable as much to Franklin as the author, Lepore doubles down on the impression in the fourth sentence. The fourth sentence, "And therein, Franklin thought, lay true nobility," is indirect discourse that is directly attributed to Franklin, followed by a fifth sentence of direct discourse.

It's a skillful sliding of perception and voice. The result is a character-determined narrative, in which the reader has both the experience of reading history and the experience of being inside the mind of Benjamin Franklin as a strong character, with internal and external desires and obstacles.

Laurel Ulrich develops a character-driven narrative by coming at her historical material from another route entirely. Ulrich's book is an example of what we have talked about previously as an enveloping structure, in which an author delves into the history of a topic and takes a reader through the field. These books generally rely on character for narrative structure, and they usually work with first-person structures, including a double first-person structure that blends memoir with history.

Her book takes that bifurcated approach in terms of character and voice, although Ulrich is not doubling the first person. One of those characters is her subject, the eighteenth-century midwife Martha Ballard. Ulrich develops Ballard as a character not through free indirect discourse — in fact, Ulrich as a matter of methodology makes it clear that she wants to present Ballard in her own writings, in the attributable and intimate speech that she left behind as a record. The other character throughout the book, however, is Ulrich herself, who remains in nearly constant dialogue with or about her subject: "Because so few New England women of her generation left writing in any form, one searches for an explanation," she writes in the introduction, for example, reminding the reader of the active role of the researcher-author. It is a role "played" by Ulrich, but it is simultaneously a role which, through the use of "one" rather than "I," the reader is also invited to take on as researcher-reader.

This is not to say that the first-person development of the researcher-author cannot also be effective. This technique is becoming relatively common in science communications, and some of the best research on the role of narrative storytelling in effective general audience communication has come out of the sciences. Here, the author-researcher becomes a kind of protagonist, on the frames of the central story, and the research subject becomes the quest narrative. The device is useful not only in character-determined narratives like Lepore's and Ulrich's but equally in plot-determined narratives. Even when the structure is more customarily plot-driven, after all, there has to be some character. A sentence has to have some subject.

Let's consider a third example, to make sure you have a clear idea how to manage author-as-character, especially in nonfiction, because for many academics this is the easiest place to begin with writing voice and character. (After all, presumably your own desires and frustrations, in respect to your research topic, are well known to you as a character.) *The Lost City of the Monkey God,* a number 1 *New York Times* nonfiction bestseller by the naturalist Douglas Preston (Grand Central, 2021), for example, uses this device effectively in a primarily plot-determined title. It's a book about the use of Lidar, the aerial radar imaging that is reshaping the field of archaeology, and Preston cleverly opens with a bird's eye view. In each successive opening paragraph, the range of vision narrows, until by the second page, he introduces himself as narrator and character.

> On February 15, 2015, I was in a conference room in the Ho-tel Papa Beto in Catacamas, Honduras, taking part in a briefing. In the following days, our team was scheduled to helicopter into an unexplored valley, known only as Target One, deep in the interior mountains of Mosquitia. The helicopter would drop us off on the banks of an unnamed river, and we would be left on our own to hack out a primitive camp in the rainforest. . . . We would be the first researchers to enter that part of Mosquitia. None of us had any idea what we would actually see on the ground, shrouded in dense jungle, in a pristine wilderness that had not seen human beings in living memory.

Preston is an experienced nonfiction writer. He opens in the first paragraph of the book with the big picture view, placing the reader in space. He zooms in, bringing the reader along with him to a location in place, and then he locates the reader in time: February 15, 2015. Keeping the focus on what's new, timely, and relevant (first researchers, not in living memory), he introduces the researcher-narrator, gives us a bit of narrative tension (no one has ever seen this place — what will they find there? Turn the page to find out), and, by making the wilderness the active subject in the last sentence ("the wilderness had not seen") turns the research subject itself into a co-character. The latter is a good strategic decision for Preston. The nature of his research topic means that there are not a lot of other characters available to him. The exploration is of an uninhabited landscape, and he does not have the kind of fact-based information about the lives of individual historical inhabitants that he would need to have those voices and experiences carry a narrative.

Finally, of course, a researcher can develop character without involving himself or herself in the narrative at all or by using author-as-character only in a preface or afterword. Benjamin Wallace's *The Billionaire's Vinegar* (Crown, 2008), for example, was a *New York Times* bestseller on the history of a bottle of wine in the collection of Thomas Jefferson. Wallace works with characterization directly, and it's worth seeing, as well, how he manages it. He writes early in the book, for example:

> It wasn't just drinking wine that interested Jefferson. . . . Now, as his horse-drawn carriage clattered along the post roads of France, he at least had a chance to see the most fabled vineyards in the world. He traveled light, bringing only a single trunk with him. Wanting to experience the real France, unfiltered by preferential treatment and unburdened by diplomatic obligations, he travelled incognito, the plan being to hire a different valet in each town, so that no one would find out who he was. Jefferson drank France in with guzzling intemperance. . . . Social observer, he walked his way into people's homes to see how they lived, ate their bread, and lay on their beds as if to rest but really to feel their softness . . . he spoke French well enough to grill laborers and cellarmasters alike. How many years before a vine started to yield good fruit? Twenty-five. Did the winemakers dung their soil? A little. . . . Away from the crush of duty and unknown to those around him, he was able to relax and reflect — and perhaps get Maria Cosway out of his mind. (10–11)

Wallace works with internal conflict and dramatic tension, sketching Jefferson as a man determined to distract himself from an ill-fated love affair through wine and travel. He works with free indirect discourse: *How many years before a vine started to yield good fruit?* He uses adverbs: "now." The effect is to position the reader in the present, to invite the reader to "see" Jefferson, and to "hear" the "clatter" of the carriage. Wallace is also using here certain forms of sentence parallelism to create sentences that "roll" just like Jefferson's carriage. Parallelism (and the breaking of parallelism) is considered in detail later in this chapter for its use in developing both character and dramatic tension. For the moment, it's just worth observing that "unfiltered by preferential treatment and unburdened by diplomatic obligations" is both strong parallelism and works with a certain repetition of stress as well as sound.

One of the things that should be immediately transparent is the considerable research — and the considerably different kind of research — that needs to go into the effective use of representational perception and free indirect discourse and the amount of narrative (and methodological) strategy that rests behind the deployment of the author-as-character in fact-based general audience writing. As a researcher, you are looking for all the same things you would usually search for in your work, and you are also looking to understand the kinds of words a research subject might deploy, for documented sources that will allow you to speak to what your subject knew, felt, or perceived, and for fact-based information (for example, about the coldness of a river) that you can use to develop character.

Finally, there is one other characterization technique that tends to work in tandem with these character-development strategies but can be used independently. It is what I call the "fish-eye lens" technique or a "character granularity." A fish-eye lens, of course, is a camera lens that takes in up to one hundred eighty degrees of the field of vision — in other words, more like what a fish sees than what humans, with our forward-facing eyes, see. The effect is to exaggerate the emphasis on perspective and place the viewer "inside" the subjectivity of the fish/camera.

If you want to create character, exaggerating perspective and placing the reader inside the subjectivity of your character is a handy device, especially if you can create that effect not by inventing what the lens captures (which, after all, would violate the nonfiction contract) but simply by giving an unusual weight to the field of vision. It basically works like this: you introduce your character by giving the character a fish-eye lens.

This does not mean you are narrating in the first person. First-person narration in nonfiction is difficult unless you have the kind of diary or memoir material that you can quote from or paraphrase that someone like Ulrich is working with. It is important to remember that, if you do have that material, paraphrase can be as effective as direct quotation, sometimes even more effective. In other words, if Mary Ann Patten left a diary (to my knowledge she did not) and if in that diary she said, "We passed today Cape Horn, and I shivered at how cold the wind was. Many of us on board were sick, myself included. I felt my stomach toss and turn," I can quote Mary Ann saying that, of course, giving her the first person.

However, I can also write: "*Neptune's Car* crept past Cape Horn at last. Mary Ann shivered in the cold wind. Her stomach was tossing and turning. Sailors around her were growing sick. Mary Ann soon would join them." I can write the passage, in other words, from Mary Ann's perspective, even in the historical third person. I can mix in that passage what I know to have been Mary Ann's perspective (the research material in the diary) with what I know also to have been other facts within her field of vision. Adding those other facts back into her field of vision is the fish-eye technique.

Let's imagine, say, that in addition to Mary Ann's diary entry, capturing her worries about the first mate, I also have a historical weather report, I have travel journals from other ships that made the passage around Cape Horn in the same period as Mary Ann describing the headland and the experience aboard a clipper, and I have the ship's log for their vessel. If I were to fish-eye that same passage, I might write:

> Mary Ann stood on the deck. It was just past dawn, and below deck at the change of watch the first mate was passing off command to Joshua. First mate Keeler worried Mary Ann. She did not trust him. She was sure that she had seen him change the compass readings. Did he mean to shipwreck them? Something had to be done. She wished Joshua were not so blinded by loyalty to his crew. As *Neptune's Car* crept past Cape Horn at last — they had fought weeks for this moment — the fog grew denser, and it was hard to make out the rocky tundra towering above them. Mary Ann shivered in the cold wind. Her stomach tossed and turned. The ship rolled under their feet, as the rollers came now straight at them. From somewhere on the foredeck came the sound of a sailor retching. Mary Ann turned to go below. She was queasy herself and felt the bile rising.

As a nonfiction writer, I have to possess a fact to back up each of those details (or use free indirect discourse and perspectival representation to pose a question). I have to know from the ship's log which direction the rollers came, and I have to know from her diary that she stood on the deck that moment. That is the creative work of granular research that writing trade nonfiction requires. However, once I have gathered up the material, what the fish-eye approach allows me to do as a writer is to establish character by giving the reader the ability to look around, in a broader field of vision, as though through Mary Ann's eyes, and to create the experience of subjectivity through the exaggeration of objective (fact-based) perspective.

What you can also see in that sample passage is that I have given Mary Ann internal and external motivations and conflicts. Mary Ann does not trust the first mate (internal motivation). Her husband doesn't take her concerns seriously, and she doesn't want to seem disloyal or create the appearance that her husband is disloyal to her crew, so she tries to stay quiet about her worries (internal conflict). She sees that the first mate is a bad guy (external motivation, protagonist versus antagonist), and she has witnessed him do something dangerous (external motivation) in a dangerous setting (external motivation). Someone must do something, but Mary Ann as a woman has no power (external conflict). And, in Mary Ann's case, the first mate is the antagonist, but Mary Ann is also being blocked by her husband, the captain Joshua (the third character). Mary Ann has to try to resolve her worries about the first mate and desire to stop him with her husband's command of the ship and his dismissing her worries.

So, to recapitulate very briefly: depending on how strongly your narrative works with character, your protagonist, antagonist, and other main characters are going to have some degree of internal and external desire and conflict that supports your narrative arc. Your characters will be of a type that we can recognize and will also be individuated. And you can work with free indirect discourse, perceptual representation, and fish-eye granularity at the sentence level to draw the reader more deeply into the world of character, as a central component of effective narrative.

Chapter 10

HOW NOT TO WRITE LIKE AN ACADEMIC

Narrative Tension

Narrative functions by tightening and loosening tension, as it is experienced by the reader, and one of the differences between a trade book and an academic book is that in a trade book each chapter functions as a mini-narrative unit.

How do we begin working with this device? How can we manage that very tricky transition between the end of one chapter and the start of another, where narrative needs to de-accelerate and re-accelerate quickly and needs to sustain a larger narrative arc? How do we manage those two particularly complex moments in a narrative — the beginning and the ending of the story, when we have to build and release tension deftly?

We could write a whole other book on the craft of writing, sentence by sentence, in narrative nonfiction, but I want to highlight here one particular sentence-level technique that functions very effectively to manage tension and pacing, especially in conjunction with character, and to make one recommendation (and one acknowledgment) at the outset.

My recommendation is that anyone faced with writing a nonfiction trade book get and read a copy of *Style and Statement,* a writing handbook by Edward Corbett and Robert Connors (Oxford University Press, 1998), which is a shortened version of their 1965 university textbook on the structure of sentence clauses and rhetorical function. I know of no other book that can teach a serious writer more about sentence-level pacing and tension.

Corbett and Connors make, if I were to sum up their handbook, two basic points: the first is that different sentence structures, in variation, have very particular and different connotative effects; the second is that creating and breaking patterns of repetition both at the sentence level and at the clause level controls pacing and emotional affect. In other words, you can create (or release) narrative tension starting with how you vary your sentences.

We all know that there are four sentence types: the simple sentence (one independent clause, with a subject, a verb, and an object if the verb is transitive), the complex sentence (one independent clause and one or more dependent clauses), the compound sentence (two independent clauses), and the compound-complex sentence (two independent clauses plus one or more dependent clauses). Complex structures are hypotactic, meaning they depend on subordination. Compound structures are paratactic; in other words, they function sequentially, with all elements at an equal level of syntactic importance. Compound sentences depend on syndeton, or connective elements, including coordinating conjunctions or punctuation such as the colon and semicolon (taking the place of a comma and a conjunction). Sentences with excessive syndeton between or among clauses use polysyndeton. Sentences with missing syndeton between or among clauses use asyndeton. If those terms all flew by too fast: read the Corbett and Connors.

—

171

If all that makes sense, then here are the takeaways most useful to you as a writer: academic writing tends to be highly hypotactic, largely because thesis as we think of it in the academy is largely about the subordination and logical sequence of truth claims. Beware of relying on hypotaxis in your general audience writing, and be sure you are at the very least working to mix paratactic and hypotactic structures. If you are struggling with writing for general audiences, try writing only with paratactic structures as an exercise. General audience writing tends to prefer paratactic structures, because they are more accessible to the general reader.

Let's look at an example of the difference. I want to be sure there are examples in this book for fact-based writers from all disciplines, and *The Atlantic* has consistently good general audience, fact-based public science writing. So I google *The Atlantic* and "science," and up pops an article from March 23, 2023, titled "One More Reason to Hate Cockroaches," by staff writer Katherine Wu. I read where she writes:

> The insects' sweet tooth should have made them easy to kill. But they outsmarted us with warp-speed evolution.
>
> In the centuries-long war between humans and cockroaches, the most bitter blow was dealt roughly 40 years ago. Tired of chasing after the pests with noxious sprays and bombs, researchers started to infuse their poisons with delicious flavors that could compel roaches to approach of their own accord, and then feast upon their own demise. The secret was sugar: Cockroaches, like us, simply couldn't resist their sweet tooth.
>
> The advent of these baits "revolutionized pest control," says Coby Schal, an entomologist at North Carolina State University. Manufacturers were sure that they had, after centuries of strife, gained a decisive upper hand. And victory was sweet.

———

But not even a decade passed before the battlefield shifted once again. In the late 1980s, the manufacturers of Combat, a popular roach bait, received a perplexed call from a pest-control operator in Florida. He'd been planting Combat all over homes for years, but suddenly, it was failing to seduce German cockroaches to their deaths. One of the company's researchers, Jules Silverman, plucked several roaches from a Gainesville apartment—and was flabbergasted to find that the insects were no longer tempted by Combat's corn syrup and instead scuttled away in disgust.

This is not simple or unsophisticated writing. This is strong general audience writing for an intelligent, non-specialist audience. Without offering an entire prose-style seminar here, let's think for a minute about how these paragraphs work and why this writing is successful—and how it is different from an academic article.

In fact, let's compare "One More Reason to Hate Cockroaches" with a recent peer-reviewed article on the same topic, "A Review of Alternative Management Tactics Employed for the Control of Various Cockroach Species (Order: Blattodea) in the USA," written by Ameya D. Gondhalekar, Arthur G. Appel, Gretchen M. Thomas, and Alvaro Romero and published in the June 2021 issue of *Insects* (12:6, 550). This is also a well-written article that successfully does all the things writing for a specialist academic audience is meant to do.

Baits alone can drastically reduce the number of cockroaches in infested apartments, but long-term suppression of cockroach populations often requires integrating other non-chemical tactics, such as sanitation, structural modifications of buildings to prevent cockroach invasion through entry points, and continuous monitoring using insect glue boards to help inform pest control interventions. Integrated approaches for cockroach control are also justified given the emergence of insecticide resistant cockroach populations, which explain control failures reported by pest management professionals (PMPs). Cockroaches, in particular the German cockroach, *Blattella germanica* (L.), have developed resistance to almost all classes of insecticides that were used for its control from the 1940s to 1990s.

More recently, resistance, or at least tolerance, to newer insecticides that are used in gel bait formulations has also been reported. Adaptive physiological responses of German cockroaches are also reflected in their development of behavioral aversion resistance to sugar-containing baits (e.g., glucose, fructose, maltose, sucrose etc.). German cockroaches that are glucose-averse do not consume the toxic bait in lethal quantities and often survive insecticide exposure. Due to these aforementioned factors, an integrated pest management (IPM) approach that emphasizes the concurrent use of chemicals with alternative control tactics continues to be considered ideal for effective control of cockroaches.

What are the differences between the public-facing writing and the academic writing? Well, there are a number of differences. One is that the specialist writing uses a number of specialist terms and acronyms: IPM, PMP, "adaptive physiological responses," "glucose-averse," and so on. Another difference is that, in general, the academic article has longer paragraphs. But look at these two examples just in terms of the two things we've been talking about here: narrative and sentence structure and variation.

The academic article is not working with narrative. There is no "story" here about any identifiable character. There is no loosening or tightening of tension. There is no struggle between characters. The academic article also uses substantially more hypotaxis and more frequent use of complex prepositional phrases and restrictive and nonrestrictive ("that" and "which") clauses. Take the first sentence quoted above:

———

Baits alone can drastically reduce the number of cockroaches in infested apartments, but long-term suppression of cockroach populations often requires integrating other non-chemical tactics, such as sanitation, structural modifications of buildings to prevent cockroach invasion through entry points, and continuous monitoring using insect glue boards to help inform pest control interventions.

Structurally, it's a compound-complex sentence: a single independent clause connected using a coordinating conjunction to an independent clause and its dependent clause. The subjects of the clauses are "baits" and "long-term suppression." The main actors in these sentences are passive. It's a perfectly well written sentence, with strong and clear parallelism, using subordination. The result is a hierarchy of ideas in efficient, discipline-appropriate, author-evacuated prose.

Compare this to "One More Reason to Hate Cockroaches." Here, there is a narrative: "the insect" versus Jules Silverman, exterminator, locked in a "centuries-long war between humans and cockroaches." There is a battlefield that shifts. There is sweetness and seduction. There are cockroaches who are "like us" — and who "like us, simply couldn't resist their sweet tooth." The cockroach as antagonist is getting characterization. Is it all a bit tongue-in-cheek? Of course. That's part of what also creates the voice in this writing. As readers we're invited into the joke. After all, what we're talking about here is a fact-based science article dancing on the edge of epic. The clauses tend to begin with subjects who are agents and actors in this drama: the insect, researchers, cockroaches, manufacturers. The sentences tend to be paratactic. Perhaps more important, the sentences are varied and build in that first paragraph to a climax. Simple sentence. Simple sentence. Simple sentence with a prepositional phrase ("In the centuries long war"). Complex sentence. Compound sentence, but this one using a colon to connect two simple sentences, a device that accelerates emphasis on the final clause: "Cockroaches, like us, simply couldn't resist their sweet tooth."

The two paragraphs that follow also work with sentence variation to build to an emphatic final sentence: "Cockroaches, like us, simply couldn't resist their sweet tooth," "victory was sweet," and an exterminator "flabbergasted to find that the insects were no longer tempted by Combat's corn syrup." Sentence variation is being used in a paragraph to build and release tension, nudging the reader along to the next paragraph, the next pithy climax. The author makes her argument by using the last sentence of each paragraph as a point of inflection and summary. In fact, when we talked early in this book about how thesis is not opposed to narrative in general audience writing but unfolds in a different manner, this would be a good example. This article is idea driven: it is an article about insect evolution and insecticide research. But narrative carries the idea forward. That is what good trade nonfiction is trying to accomplish.

Let's look at one more example of working effectively with sentence variation — an example that is a bit more dramatic, in case you're not seeing the climaxes in Wu's paragraphs or the role sentence variation can play in controlling dramatic tension. There is no way to put this politely: if you would like to see an orgasm in writing, achieved primarily through the use of sentence (and clause) variation, consider this paragraph from M. F. K. Fisher's essay "Once a Tramp, Always," published in the *New Yorker* as long ago as August 31, 1968, under the original title "Notes on Cravings."

> I have some of the same twinges of basic craving for those salty gnarled little nuts from Hawaii as the ones I keep ruthlessly at bay for the vulgar fried potatoes and the costly fish eggs. Just writing of

my small steady passion for them makes my mouth water in a reassuringly controlled way, and I am glad there are dozens of jars of them in the local goodies shoppe, for me not to buy. . . . The last time I ate one was about four months ago, in New York. I surprised my *belle-soeur* and almost embarrassed myself by letting a small moan escape me when she put a bowl of them beside my chair; they were beautiful — so lumpy, Macadamian, salty, golden! And I ate one, to save face. One.

If you find yourself at the end of a chapter and another cliffhanger seems overdone, remember that you can create propulsive narrative with sentence variation as a device to build and release dramatic tension.

You can also work with sentence structure, especially combined with diction, to create voice. Voice is a way of leveraging all of the silent decisions we get to make as writers about word choice, sentence patterns, sentence structures, to create the sense of a writer-as-character behind that story. Lepore works, as we saw in the earlier example, effectively with diction, simply by placing words that to a modern ear sound archaic (and, therefore, authentically original to an eighteenth-century character) in the context of free indirect discourse. It creates an experience of "hearing" Benjamin Franklin without actually ascribing to Franklin any speech. A paragraph written in all compound-complex sentences, with "thesaurus words," will sound convincingly professorial. The use of all simple sentences, on the other hand, will sound childlike. A book like *Dick and Jane,* for example, is clearly aimed at either very young or very inexperienced readers.

Paragraphs that sparingly use hypotaxis and then primarily for roiling, confused interior thoughts, followed by crisp paratactic active sentences, function effectively to create a sense of character subjectivity, followed by narrative tension, that propel a story forward.

———

This is a formula that, if you're working on your first trade book, you can play around with if you get the sense the narrative is lagging.

You can also control pacing with something as simple as a conjunction. It's worth noticing, for example, the use of asyndeton — the deliberate omission of conjunctions — in Fisher's excited nut appreciation: "so lumpy, Macadamian, salty, golden." It is how she creates that effect of climax.

Standard English puts a conjunction at the end of items in a series; omitting to do so creates a sense of immediacy and urgency and voice. It's also a useful trick to remember as you are learning to work with the spooling and unspooling of narrative tension. Again, my best advice is simply to go read Corbett and Connors carefully. Do the imitation exercises in the back, because you will learn a huge amount by breaking effective writing down in a rhetorical analysis and imitating it as an exercise in pacing and voice. If you are stuck because your editor is coming back at you saying that your writing is still too academic, ask your agent or editor for some representative texts they admire, do a rhetorical analysis, do an imitation, and then go back to your writing and see if you can incorporate some of those patterns of variation. If your chapter doesn't have a strong narrative climax at the end, you can try working instead with a character climax or with a straightforward prose climax focused on some salient detail that carries over from one chapter to the next.

If sentence types and variation are the pattern at the sentence and paragraph level, also be aware that Corbett and Connors have a good deal to say as well about precisely how to work with repetition and variation at the clause level. To some extent, all story — from the narrative arc to the sentence level — is about creating certain expectations through repetition and then breaking those expectations through variation. That's at the core of creating dramatic tension in a paragraph with sentence variation, and just be aware that you can also work with this kind of pacing at the clause level. Again, summarizing shamelessly here, Corbett and Connors make the basic point that you can have repetition at the beginning of successive clauses, at the ending of successive clauses, at the beginning of one clause and the end of another, or vice versa. Anaphora, epistrophe (or epiphora), anadiplosis, and so on, if you're looking for the classical terms. So, for example, "Tyger," a poem by William Blake, uses anaphora: "What the hammer? what the chain? / In what furnace was thy brain? / What the anvil? what dread grasp / Dare its deadly terrors clasp?" Dr. Martin Luther King's "I Have a Dream" speech, delivered at the March on Washington in August 1963, on the other hand, uses epistrophe: "With this faith we will be able to work together, to pray together, to struggle together, to go to jail together, to stand up for freedom together, knowing that we will be free one day."

Both devices have slightly different rhetorical effects. Anaphora tends to be more inviting. Epistrophe tends to be more emphatic and emotional. My point is simply that you want to be aware of these devices and the ways in which you can learn to work with them, both in terms of writing character and creating narrative. You cannot as a nonfiction writer put words into the mouth of your historical figure or ascribe to your character feelings that you do not have documentary evidence they felt and recorded. There is nothing, however, in the nonfiction contract that prevents you from taking fact-based material and presenting it to a reader, to an emotional effect, using either sentence variation or clause repetition. You can create the experience of a character's emotion indirectly (rhetorically) and not only directly (narratively), and be aware as well that the stronger the pattern of repetition you create, the more dramatic the eventual, well-placed break in the pattern becomes for a reader.

You can also try, of course, working with initial conjunctions, starting your sentences with "and" or "but," for example. Normally, this would be discouraged in formal standard English. I've spent a lifetime nagging freshmen composition students not to do it. And I freely admit to doing it myself. Why? Because it's effective. The voice it creates is lighter, more chatty, more intimate. We break up our sentences "incorrectly," we move from thought to thought without cumbersome (and more correct) therefore's and however's in intimate circles, when we are talking frankly among equals. Fragments selectively (and judiciously) used can perform the same function. "Breaking" the formal rules of grammar or usage, in other words, can be a silent way of creating character, especially author-as-character.

Finally, one last piece of advice about what writing does not include as a general audience writing strategy. As you will recall, we talked early in this book about the trade book as a title in which the reader is given far broader scope to do the narrative work (and receive the narrative satisfaction) of putting together themes, topoi, and ideas. I've mentioned the pregnant pause and "writing the gap." These are two slightly different techniques. Both are central to your ability to tighten and release narrative tension in an arc.

The pregnant pause is exactly what we mean by that expression in daily idiom: the moment where silence speaks and gestates meaning. Stand-up comedy relies on it. So do horror novels. In a film like *Jaws,* a lot of the narrative weight is famously carried by that wordless soundtrack (and your version of the soundtrack as a writer is sentence variation and control of clauses). In Canadian politics, there is a famous moment from 2013, easily found on YouTube for some cringeworthy viewing, when Rob Ford, then the mayor of Toronto, was asked by a council member on camera whether he had purchased illegal drugs in the past two years. The mayor ultimately answered "Yes, I have," but it was the eight-second pause that did the talking. In that silence, stunned journalists could read a whole story about internal motivation and conflict and character. There was a good neuroscience-informed discussion of Ford's voluminous speechlessness published in *PLOS One* (December 23, 2015) under the title "Never Say No . . . How the Brain Interprets the Pregnant Pause in Conversation" that I recommend to the curious.

Writing the gap (also called writing the gutter) is a slightly different approach to working with silences in a text as a narrative pacing and character development device, borrowing from the world of graphic novels. If you want a more detailed overview about this, I give an entire lecture on narrative silence in a video course called "Writing Creative Nonfiction" (The Great Courses, 2012). "Writing the gap" is a term and technique I am borrowing here from the graphic novelist Scott McCloud, whose book *Understanding Comics* (William Morrow, 1993) I recommend highly.

Think about how graphic novels work by frames. The space between the frames is the gutter, and, in order to create narrative, the writer needs to write the gap—find a way, in other words, to set up the narrative so that it jumps from one frame to the next. As a nonfiction writer, you can work with this technique between paragraphs or sections, but you ultimately need to work with it or with some other comparable technique to write the gap between chapters. McCloud offers numerous examples of how you can use narrative tension between frames to create a story that the reader completes, but you can see the same thing by looking at any newspaper comic strip or graphic novel. In one frame something is about to happen.

In the next frame, the consequences of what has happened are depicted. There is a shift in perspective between narrative moments. There is generally as well a shift in proximity, moving from close up to a distant view, or vice versa. Again, I encourage anyone serious about learning to write narrative to read McCloud, who says this and a great deal more of value.

The key point, though, is that between those two frames, there is a gap that is narrated by implication only. The reader is left to infer and to "write" for him or herself the narrative progression: the attacker has harmed his victim. Lucy has pulled the football away from Charlie. We see the cause, and we see the effect. There is no need to narrate the actual event. In fact, not positively narrating the event—much like the restraint I spoke about using as a deliberate "horror" factor in writing about the Holocaust—is more dramatically effective. The reader fills that gap with his or her own images, more specific to that reader's engagement with the story and the characters than yours could ever have been, and becomes an active participant in the construction of the narrative arc. General audience writing depends on this, and in this is starkly different from what academic writing asks of an author. Again: get out of the way of your reader and your story.

You can see, I hope, the implication for writing narrative nonfiction: one way to think about chapters is to think about them as the narrative blocks in a panel and to think about the gap between panels as a chapter break. This is an excellent visualization of how you want to think about chapters as ending on a moment of narrative tension that is propulsive and picking up after the gap with another aspect of that unresolved narrative tension. However, you can also think about building narrative or character within a chapter using this technique of juxtaposition. Essentially, you offer one moment of, say, character, perhaps using a fish-eye technique to create sub-jective intensity. You write a gap, and then you follow up with the (unspoken but implied) narrative consequence.

And if these are techniques for building narrative tension and either releasing that tension or carrying it over the gap between sections or chapters, just a final word about how to begin chapters and, indeed, books for general readers: you want to start with something that makes a reader want to know more about something. Begin with something incongruous. Begin with character. And begin with conflict. The classically brilliant and oft-cited example of this is the opening line of Gabriel García Márquez's novel *One Hundred Years of Solitude* (Harper & Row, 1970): "Many years later, as he faced the firing squad, Colonel Aureliano Buendía was to remember that distant afternoon when his father took him to discover ice." What the hell, the reader immediately wants to know. Who is this colonel? Why is he in front of a firing squad? What is his childhood memory about ice? And why is he thinking of that now? In one sentence, García Márquez manages to set in motion an entire narrative arc.

That is the role of your chapter openers (even if you cannot get it into one brilliant sentence) and that is the function as well of your narrative summary. We cannot all be García Márquez, so again, it's perfectly all right to think of this as a matter of a paragraph or two at the start of a chapter (or the start of a book), rather than one sentence. What you want to set in motion, however, is the same internal narrative for each chapter, and you want each chapter to sustain an overarching narrative arc across the gaps. That is what you're looking to do in your chapter summaries, and it's also what you want to communicate in your sample chapter.

And at the end of a book, you need to give the reader the satisfaction of an organic resolution. Colonel Buendía will face the firing

—

squad, and we will know about the ice his father showed him. Or there will be some other ending equally satisfying. (No spoilers!) The tension will be released. The threads will untangle. The clock will wind down and go silent. As you are researching, keep in mind that one of the neatest ways to open and end a story is to remember that all narratives can be circular, in some sense, and to look for a recursive moment or image that brings the reader (even if not the character) full circle. You can use sentence-level strategies to heighten and release that tension, and you can use the fish-eye lens of character as an effective movement from narrative to interiority. One of the reasons why the enveloping narrative is attractive for first-time trade authors is that it offers a built-in recursive structure and a character opening and closing, which many writers find easier to manage at the beginning than zero-to-sixty narrative pacing.

Chapter 11

WRITING NARRATIVE NONFICTION
Why Bestsellers Sell

How do we put all this together? The answer is as simple as it is maddening: we just keep looking at examples of writing done well, we keep learning. As I put the finishing touches on this book, I look at the *New York Times* nonfiction bestseller list. There, in May 2023, is Isabel Wilkerson's nonfiction work *Caste: The Origin of Our Discontents* (Random House, 2020). It's been there for six weeks running. Why, I wonder?

So I open to a page and begin reading. It's there, of course, because Wilkerson is a good trade writer. She comes from a long background in journalism and narrative nonfiction. She has a big idea. It's relevant, sadly; it's timely. I read:

> The inspector trained his infrared lens onto a misshapen bow in the ceiling, an invisible beam of light searching the layers of lath to test what the eye could not see. The house had been built generations ago, and I had noticed the slightest welt in a corner of plaster in a spare room and had chalked it up to idiosyncrasy. Over time, the welt in the ceiling became a wave that widened and bulged despite the new roof. It had been building beyond perception for years. An

---

old house is its own kind of devotional, a dowager aunt with a story to be coaxed out of her, a mystery, a series of interlocking puzzles awaiting solution. Why is this soffit tucked into the southeast corner of an eave? What is behind this discolored patch of brick? With an old house, the work is never done, and you don't expect it to be.

America is an old house.

That's good, smart writing. Interesting. There is a light touch in how she develops the author-as-character: just one, single "I" conjures up a world of do-it-yourself home renovations. We start in the fish-eye view of the inspector: the ceiling. Only later do we learn of the woman who had noticed it and thought to ask for the inspection. I am immediately sympathetic, feel rapport with Wilkerson. After all, I, too, have owned a home with collapsing plaster. Most of the rapport is built through voice, though, a combination of sentence variation and a consciousness of a storyteller who is storytelling, coaxing the tale out of that dowager aunt. The questions edge us toward free indirect discourse, though we think we know who is speaking. And look, sentence variation, with the weight crashing down on one simple sentence (and the thesis): America.

I turn to *The Body Keeps the Score* (Penguin, 2015). More than two hundred weeks now on the *New York Times* list. This is not a good comp anymore for anyone. Van der Kolk's title has clearly entered the overly aspirational firmament. I remind myself, however, that when it was first published it did not immediately receive this recognition. Market timing. It grew into its relevance. I read:

> As the session was drawing to a close, I did what doctors typically do: I focused on the one part of Tom's story that I thought I understood — his nightmares. . . . When he returned for his appointment, I eagerly asked Tom how the medicines had worked.

He told me he hadn't taken any of the pills. Trying to conceal my irritation, I asked him why. "I realized that if I take the pills and the nightmares go away," he replied, "I will have abandoned my friends, and their deaths will have been in vain. I need to be a living memorial to my friends who died in Vietnam." I was stunned: Tom's loyalty to the dead was keeping him from living his life. . . . How had that happened, and what could be done about it? (2)

I also see why this book has struck a chord with so many readers. Dr. van der Kolk has turned himself into a character, and it's one that's easy to like. Here's a man with great expertise and knowledge, offering a fireside chat that feels straight from the heart and self-reflective. He's telling a history of how he's changed as a doctor (a hint of a circular narrative), how the medical profession has changed, and how "we" the readers can change our life stories. Author-as-character organizing and framing a series of enveloping stories, and at the center of this particular Russian doll is you, whoever you may be. "You, whoever you may be" is a big audience.

Reading books like the one you want to write, in other words, is from here the best way forward. Learn, borrow. Then, all that's left is to write your sample chapter and complete your book proposal. To do that, you will likely need to do some research — the right kind of research to give a snapshot of narrative.

The function of the narrative arc in general audience chapters is to make each chapter satisfying to read as a unit and to create those entry and exit points. Compelling chapters make it easy to pick the narrative back up and hard to put the book down. I am mulling what I will do in a sample chapter for the Mary Ann Patten biography. I am mulling, more specifically, what research I will need to do to write it — and that research, as I've said before, might not be the research you think it would be unless you know that the fish eye and free indirect discourse and character perception are techniques of trade writing.

I don't need to know more about the Gold Rush or where *Neptune's Car,* their ship, was constructed. That is information for later. Now, I need to know more about what exactly the inside of a clipper ship looked like in this time period. I need to have a sense of what kind of wind and weather forces an extreme clipper could reasonably withstand and what kind of shoes were worn (or not worn) by sailors in the 1860s. I need to understand what a storm would have looked like (drawn from first-hand accounts and historical material, if possible), and I need to be able to describe — based on historical fact — what it was like to wake up in Antarctica.

What you'll notice is that I am primarily looking at this point for concrete, research-based details (nonfiction) that I can use to fill out my narrative structure. The "contract" of narrative nonfiction is that, as long as all the details are fact-based, we can deploy the devices of narrative, and the old adage of narrative is "show, don't tell." I find that adage a bit hackneyed, and I prefer to think of it as a matter of granularity. If my narrative arc is the telescopic, I also want to counterbalance that with the microscopic.

Thinking about where to find these facts efficiently — and without falling into the temptation of over-researching — can require some lateral thinking. Obviously, you can look for this information in academic monographs on these topics, and you can look in libraries, archives, or online for historical records and journals. But you will often, either now or later in writing the manuscript, find that you have to think a bit creatively about where you might find information when the location isn't obvious.

When I was writing *The Widow Clicquot,* for example, I was running into some research dead-ends when it came to describing the widow herself. It was tough to develop character without being able to give some detail about how others saw her and what her home, for example, looked like. In the end, I found the first-hand descriptions by trawling through nineteenth-century travel journals written by American tourists in France, where she was a tourist attraction. It was just the odd paragraph, and I came upon the first one by chance. After, it was obvious that this was where I always should have been looking.

When I was writing a biography of Eliza Hamilton, wife of Alexander Hamilton, and puzzling over what really happened in Alexander Hamilton's self-confessed affair with Maria Reynolds and why certain things didn't add up, I found the piece I needed not in any Hamilton material but in a footnote to the collected works of his arch rival, Thomas Jefferson. In retrospect, it seemed obvious that, if I wanted to hear the other side of an argument, the papers of someone looking to undercut Hamilton's account would be a good place to look, but it took me longer to figure that out than I care to admit. I also found the most crucial material in some archival records related to the Hamilton family women — having nothing to do with politics or much at all apart from household sisterly gossip — in a collection of letters coming up for auction and advertised in the newspaper. I wrote to the auction house, who kindly wrote to the sellers, who allowed me to read those letters as a group before they were split up and went off, separately, to private individual collections.

All of which is to say, by all means look in the usual places and do the keyword searches, but it's also worth pausing to remember that keyword searches leave out a great deal and to think about the kinds of places information might appear that our algorithms and research habits don't readily capture. And it's worth asking whether unusual materials exist and whether you can see them.

What next? Where do you go from here? What happens once you have a complete book proposal, one you've crafted and revised, one that includes your sample chapter? You're ready to get an agent (if you're going that route) and to begin shopping your proposal.

Once you have a complete draft of your book proposal, you are ready to think about the question of whether you want to work with a literary agent or not. This is a question that depends, to a large extent, on where you hope to publish your general audience title, and there are advantages and disadvantages of the different options. If you are going to publish with one of the Big Five, however, agents are not optional. Big Five publishing houses work through agents only.

Agents work primarily on commission. When you get an agent, he or she will take a percentage of your royalties. That will include your advance — your "advance on royalties." This will be forever on that piece of intellectual property. Fifteen percent is the industry standard. In your contract, your royalties will be assigned and paid to your agency, your agent will deduct his or her cut, and you will be paid by the agency on the balance due.

Since agents primarily work on commission or some combination of commission and a base salary, they are only going to agree to represent work that is marketable. They know what is marketable, because selling books to publishers and editors is what they do. For the Big Five publishers, agents perform the important work of filtering out big books from titles that are not market competitive. So, if you were a Big Five editor, someone who otherwise would receive hundreds of queries of varying quality, from sometimes emotional authors, why would you not work only through an agent? An editor knows that if someone is "repped" (represented), that book proposal has already been professionally vetted by someone who understands the current market.

If you're going to publish with the Big Five, then: agent required. In order to get an agent, you need a good book proposal. It doesn't have to be perfect. But the book proposal to get an agent does need to be very solid. Most agents will help you fine tune and hone your book proposal before taking it out for sale, but your proposal needs to be ninety percent of the way there in order to get an agent.

Your agent will also negotiate your contract, knowing what is reasonable and what's not and acting as your de facto attorney, and he or she will mediate any issues that come up between a writer and a publisher. Agents are a buffer. They are also coaches. If you have a great agent, he or she will also act as a career adviser, steering you toward good opportunities and telling you bluntly when something simply is not a general audience topic. If you have a concern, you should always first punt it to your agent. Like a literary realtor, they take emotion out of the deal, and writing tends to get emotional.

Things are different outside the Big Five. It is possible to approach the trade lists of university publishers and the editors at some of the smaller independent presses on your own, without an agent. Some of the most prestigious independent presses, more literary houses like Graywolf, for example, limit unsolicited submissions to certain open submission periods or to prize submissions. Occasionally you will be charged a reading fee to cover the cost of the editor's readings. Personally, I find that outrageous, but I can also see that for those presses the costs of open submissions are substantial. You have to decide how you feel about it. Unnamed Press, an excellent small press publishing narrative nonfiction, considers unrepresented submissions, but authors must query with a letter be-fore sending a proposal. Obviously that query letter (and the narra-tive summary as a key paragraph) needs to be stellar. If they are not interested, they will not respond to the query letter. So there are a couple of different models you might encounter.

If you have an academic appointment and you know you only want to publish on the trade lists of university presses, and if you feel you can put together a strong book proposal on your own, I'm not entirely persuaded of the advantage of an agent. The cultures of the academy and the university press are pretty well aligned, and there don't tend to be a lot of communication pitfalls. If I were an academic looking to move into trade publishing at one of the smaller independent presses, however, I would find the argument for an agent stronger. Those cultures are not as well aligned, and at small independent presses, where the publicity budgets are less robust, a lot more depends on the marketing efforts of the author. An agent is a good source of guidance. If I knew that I was ultimately thinking I'd like to place a title with a Big Five publisher, I'd look for an agent earlier rather than later given that for a Big Five book contract agents are required. If I knew that I was looking for an academic exit plan, for any reason, and considering trade writing as an alt-academic ca-reer, I'd also look for an agent early, on the theory that I would need as much career guidance as I could solicit. Otherwise, it's a personal decision, and reasonable people can go in either direction.

Finding an agent is also going to involve some research. Different agents have different specializations, and this part can be frustrat-ing, because you need to be able to articulate for yourself where your book "fits" into a market you don't yet know in order to identify which agents are most likely to be interested in your book proposal. The place to start is, again, *Publisher's Marketplace* (www.publishersmarketplace.com). You can research certain book sales, book trends, and agents. Once you have a list of thirty names, rank them in tiers — your top ten, your second ten, your third ten — and go read the websites of your top ten agents. Find out whether they allow multiple submissions and understand you will send a proposal to more than one agent at a time. Most agents do, but there are some who don't.

Personally, I'd start only with agents that do accept multiple proposals and move any agent who doesn't accept multiple submissions down to a lower-priority tier, because there's always an element of chance and luck in finding an agent, and I wouldn't want to tie myself up waiting for one individual who might know my project is a hard pass within minutes — but take weeks (or more) to tell me so. Find out what they say they are looking for in a proposal. Double-check that they are still working in the area of your proposal. Then, when you have a list of ten agents that tick all the boxes, draft a standard query email — short, sweet, succinct.

I'd use a formula something along these lines.

> Dear [Agent Name], I have been researching agents to represent my nonfiction book proposal, and I see you represent books in this area. You were recommended to me by X Colleague [if appropriate]. I notice you are the agent for Y Book, which I think will interest a similar demographic [if appropriate].
>
> My proposed title, [snazzy title of your book], is Z genre [if you're not sure, "adult nonfiction"] and the story of [give in one or two sentences — not more — your book pitch].
>
> [If you are direct submitting unrepresented to a publishing house requiring only a letter before submitting a proposal, give your 4–6 sentence, one short-to-medium pitch here. Otherwise, omit and attach the proposal to the email.]

———

I am a professor of W [or your academic affiliation, as appropriate] at University V. [Then one sentence here on your author platform or experience reaching general audiences.]

Enclosed please find a book proposal [if appropriate], about which I would be pleased to talk further. I am submitting to a small number of agents at this time, but I hope this project might interest you especially.

[Courteous closing, signature]

And that's it. Attach your proposal as a PDF. You do not want the format to be scrambled or the agent to be unable to open the file if you get far enough to tempt one to open and read it. Under no circumstances should this query letter go more than a page (or the email equivalent). It's not necessary, and being long-winded will not help. The most important part of this letter is paragraph two (and, if relevant, paragraph three), your logline and book pitch. This is the part you want to spend time crafting.

How do you craft a logline and pitch? You need a one- to two-sentence pitch. To write this, go back to your narrative summary and try to identify the narrative kernel. I found the advice of my film agent useful in thinking about these two sentences. In the film industry, that first sentence is known as the logline, and you have seen them before, anytime you've scrolled through the list of movies showing at your local theater and read the brief teaser descriptions. Those are loglines, and that is what you're looking to replicate in the first sentence of your book pitch.

Here are some famous examples of loglines. *The Godfather:* "Aging patriarch of an organized crime dynasty transfers control of his clandestine empire to his reluctant son." *Forrest Gump:* "Forrest Gump, while not intelligent, has accidentally been present at many

historic moments, but his true love, Jenny Curran, eludes him."
Titanic: "Two star-crossed lovers fall in love on the maiden voyage
of the *Titanic* and struggle to survive as the doomed ship sinks into
the Atlantic Ocean."

The second sentence of your pitch is the shortest sentence you
can come up with that explains your project's timeliness and relevance. You are looking for a relatively simple sentence here. This is
not the place to demonstrate that you know how to construct compound-complex sentences and are a master of hypotaxis.

If you're looking for examples directly related to nonfiction publications, I recommend reading reviews of books similar to your
proposed title in the *Library Journal* or *Kirkus Reviews.* Once, at the
very beginning of my transition to writing for general audiences, I
worked as an anonymous reviewer for *Kirkus.* It was incredibly useful experience in learning both the book market and how to recognize and articulate the narrative core of a nonfiction work, because
what reviewers are specifically asked to do in those reviews is to sum
up a book's arc in about two hundred and fifty words.

Library Journal, however, has taken the form to an even more extreme and useful conclusion: each of their reviews ends with a one-
or two-sentence "verdict," which is essentially a logline and a pitch
rolled into one. As I am writing this, their current reviews include
verdicts such as: "A rapturous biography for casual readers. This in-
depth analysis of one of the United States' richest families reveals a
behind-the-scenes legacy of love and generosity" (Reginato,
Growing Up Getty, biography). Or: "An important and highly read-
able addition to the history of crime and sexual politics in America
that will be of interest to historians, women-focused history researchers, sociologists, and fans of true crime" (Sweet, *The Sewing
Girl's Crime,* history). You'll notice that in my final book proposal for

---

the Mary Ann Patten project the first sentence of my narrative summary is essentially a logline and pitch opener: "A new contribution to Antarctic extreme adventure and women's historical biography from Tilar J. Mazzeo, author of the *New York Times* bestselling *Widow Clicquot, Irena's Children, Hotel on Place Vendôme.*"

You could do worse than to emulate these *Library Journal* verdicts if you're looking to craft a succinct pitch for your trade title (although I'd leave out evaluations like "rapturous"), and *Kirkus* reviews are a good model for how to write a short narrative summary. Just remember that you're looking for not more than one short sentence that describes the book's topic and not more than one short sentence (or clause) that states its relevance. Or you can do both in one sentence. Both *Kirkus* and *Library Journal* in general are excellent ways to get the feel for how the publishing industry talks about titles and what it considers worth highlighting.

You send in your proposal to an agent. You send your short and snazzy cover letter. You wait. And one day an agent writes you back and tells you this is a great book idea, and she would be happy to discuss representing you. Congratulations! From here, you will sign a representation agreement with your agent, for something like the industry standard of fifteen percent. Once you have found an agent, you should expect to receive editorial feedback on your book proposal, and for first-time authors it is not uncommon that you will be asked to do a major revision of your book proposal before an agent "takes it out," which means submitting it to publishers. Be prepared for this and remember that, if you are asked to do a revision, even a major revision, this is what you were trying to achieve: you are now being given the benefit of expert advice and mentorship to learn to do the thing you don't yet know how to do, at an up-front cost of nothing. I have seen people get to this stage, get defensive about revisions, and blow up the entire deal that they had spent months trying to work out.

When you have a book proposal that you and your agent both feel is strong and marketable, your agent will begin to circulate your book proposal to publishers, and behind the scenes, your agent generally is doing quite a lot of networking on your behalf. Agents and editors frequently meet for lunches where they go over a proposal or a handful of proposals in which an editor is interested, and from here the process is a lot like selling a house. Your book is the house, the editors are the potential buyers, and your agent—with apologies to agents everywhere for this metaphor—is your real-estate broker.

If an editor wants to make an offer on your book proposal, they will let your agent know that they will be taking the proposal to their acquisitions meeting. There are various formulations of this meeting. At Big Five trade houses, the meetings are large and quite formal. At independent presses, this might be an editor popping into the publisher's office. The acquiring editor—your editor!—will research "comps" and do a "P&L" (profit-and-loss projection). One way or the other, the editor, the publisher, and the marketing team will read and discuss your proposal and the P&L, make some educated guesses on how many copies of your book they believe they can sell, and from there work backward to what they are willing to offer as an advance, which as you'll recall is an advance on royalties.

Sometimes an editor will ask to set up a call with you and your agent. I've had this happen maybe fifty percent of the time, and you'll generally be asked how you found your topic, where the materials for the research are, and to say more about how you imagine the narrative arc and character unfolding. If you're not sure how to prepare for this, ask your agent, but at the very least I'd recommend doing some research about the publishing house and the editor to see what kind of stories he or she tends to acquire and what segment of the book market, if any, they specialize in. Even if that goes well, it's still possible that occasionally sales or marketing will not support the acquisition or the editor will decide the narrative arc isn't a good fit for their market, and in those cases an offer will not be forthcoming. Generally, however, once you get to this stage, an offer of a book contract and an advance is likely.

Once an editor tells your agent that he or she is planning to make an offer or presents an offer, your agent will contact all the other editors who have expressed interest in your book. If those editors are also interested in making an offer, you might find yourself in the highly desirable situation known as "going to auction" or a call for "best bids." This is the equivalent of multiple offers when you're selling a home, and it is relatively rare in the publishing world. I have published seven and gone under contract now for eight trade nonfiction titles, all with Big Five imprints, and only twice in my career has a book gone to best bids. One was a four-way auction for the Mary Ann Patten project, and one was a three-way auction for the book that was published as *Irena's Children* (Gallery, 2017). Books that go to auction typically command above-average advances. More typically, though, what happens is your agent receives an offer, there is only one, and from there the agent and the editor start hammering out a deal.

That deal will include the amount of the advance, the royalties, the delivery date, and the rights as the essential details. The delivery date will generally be the date in your book proposal, unless the editor is asking for an adjustment for particular marketing reasons, and you'll be involved in this conversation. The royalties are generally standard, but your agent might try to get certain terms upgraded. You will be updated by your agent, but here you want to just let your agent do the best he or she can on standard terms. The rights will distinguish between those contracted, those shared, and those reserved. Reserved rights are those that you continue to own, and, in most cases, this will be film and television rights and sometimes foreign rights. It's pretty typical if you're based in North America to receive an offer for sale of either North American rights (the United States and Canada) or world rights in English (world-wide English language). British publishers generally offer either United Kingdom and Commonwealth rights or world English. It's pretty typical for a publisher to want to include "first serial," which is the right to excerpt the book in a major magazine, and audio-book rights. Again, just let your agent do his or her magic. Agents have every incentive to want to negotiate the best deal possible.

You have an offer. It's an undeniably exciting moment. Your agent will telephone or sometimes send you an email with the title: "Offer!" There will be some back and forth about terms and conditions. You'll come to a deal, and within the first day or two the essentials will be written up in a one-page agreement known as a "deal memo." The actual contract will take weeks or months to come in many cases, as the attorneys hash out whatever the attorneys find to hash out in a boilerplate document. Don't stress. The deal memo is the deal. Let the rest of it roll over you like water.

There are, however, before you finish that negotiation, two things you want to think about and possibly negotiate or have your agent negotiate. You want to negotiate anything that is important to you before the deal memo. And there is one big contract caveat.

Let's start with the caveat. This item is not a negotiating point, but it is crucial. Very often in trade contracts these days you will find a morals clause. This is normal (though not without controversy) and generally not negotiable. Read it, because it matters. It will be in the actual contract and not in the deal memo. This contract clause basically says that if you do (or are discovered to have done) any-thing to destroy your moral reputation (the basis of your author platform), the publisher can cancel the contract — and require the re-turn of advances.

We have been accustomed in academics, if we are tenured, to the idea that as long as we are not seducing students or committing aca-demic-integrity violations, such as plagiarism, our positions are se-cure. We have the protections of academic freedom to say whatever we like, no matter who finds it offensive, although there can cer-tainly be both inflicted and self-inflicted reputational harms inside the academy. But for those of us who have been privileged enough to be tenured, our experience of the institution has been one of consid-erable freedom of expression.

That is not true in the world of trade publishing. If you go on social media at 2 a.m. and write some thoughtless comment that is morally offensive (to someone?) or publicly condemned (by some number of people?), even if at 2:10 a.m. you think better of it and delete it, your publisher is reserving the right, should someone screenshot and share that post, to cancel your book contract on the grounds that your conduct has harmed sales and the value of any intellectual property you might produce. I don't want to stoke para-noia here, but, seriously: don't. You are now a public figure, entering a public sphere. That is the transition you are making.

Be prepared for anything you publish (which is to say: post on-line or are recorded as saying) to be scrutinized, and act accordingly. Remember that being recorded these days can include in the class-room, as chilling as we might find that. A little paranoia is probably not unwarranted. If your First Amendment rights are a hill you're prepared to die on, that's completely your prerogative. It's your publisher's prerogative to cancel your book contract.

Keep in mind that prior content can come back and bite you. In theory, the internet is forever. In practice, most of us are not culturally visible enough for our old social media posts to have been archived. Before you send off your book proposal, do a thorough search of your name (including images). Copyright law is complex and varies hugely between the United States and the European Union in particular, but in cases where you own the intellectual property (as with a social media post you authored), you can generally either delete the content or request that it be taken down. There are any number of online apps that you can use as well to locate and scrub content that might negatively affect your reputation. Two particularly good (paid) ones are Optery and Delete Me. Remember that clicking on something moves it up the algorithm and makes it more likely to appear in a search. Do not repeatedly click on an item unless you want to make it more visible. If something cannot be removed and actually matters (and Rate My Professor reviews, as anonymous third-party opinions, no matter how annoying they are, do not matter), keep in mind that the best way to make internet content invisible is to bury it under newer and more relevant content that you find more palatable.

One way or the other, morals clauses are the norm, and now is your chance to go back through your social media and delete anything as yet unarchived that might be misconstrued. Keep it respectful, keep it positive, keep it clean, and if you wouldn't want to see it on the front page of the *New York Times,* get rid of it before you go public. Keep in mind that your home address might rank among the things you would not want to be publicly searchable once you have fifty thousand readers. Offer another address on your webpage, either a post office box, your campus address, or the address of your agent.

Finally, there are two special items of the trade book contract that you may want to consider negotiating as an academic author: source notes and image licenses.

For academics, source notes can be a cause of anxiety. Let's be frank about the reality: running notes — that is to say, the superscript numbers at the end of a sentence in the text to flag a citation — are generally not allowed in a Big Five trade title. On the trade list of an academic press or with an independent small publisher, you may be able to negotiate this, but for a trade title anywhere else it is highly unlikely to be supported. Negotiating note numbers in a Big Five trade contract is probably just using capital that you'd be wiser spending elsewhere. The problem is that general readers find these notes intrusive and annoying. It comes across as too academic for those readers.

Consider whether you really need notes with superscript numbers and why. There is a perfectly reasonable compromise, and my advice is that this is not a hill to die on. In this approach, you probably will be allowed to have some silent catch-phrase endnotes — notes that are unmarked in the running text but are collected in a separate section at the end of the book with catch phrases from the relevant sentence. However, if you want these, you must negotiate them in the contract in advance (and as an academic you should). They will be printed in smaller type at the back of the book. They will include the bibliographic citation only, without commentary. The National Endowment for the Humanities, if you are on the humanities side of the cathedral, accepts in their application process for the Public Scholars fellowships that footnotes are typically not part of a public-facing title, but catch-phrase notes are a good alternative. You will probably still be asked to trim them. Agree graciously.

The other option is the system that I've used here in this book, where I've tried in the running text to give enough bibliographic information for you to easily locate the reference source should you want it. These days, if you have the title of an article or a book and the snippet of any quotation from it, and use some basic Boolean logic in your search terms, the material will turn up in an internet query immediately, so that note citations are increasingly a hangover from a time when information about sources was stored only in a card catalogue and dusty library stacks, and not keyword searchable on a laptop computer. All of the sources in this book are available online to a reader as full text. What has seemed to me important is the acknowledgment of source material, not the cataloging of it.

You will probably be asked at some point, as well, whether you are contracting to include images in your book. If you are, state this in your book proposal. Generally, there should be a last paragraph or some bullet points giving your delivery date, a word count, and the number of images you plan to include. You may find that you are encouraged to include images (or more images) in your manuscript, especially if your title has a strong historical or character-driven component. Resist the temptation to overpromise on images, because they can be a lot of work and cost you a fair bit of money.

The cost of licensing the cover art is the press's responsibility, but licensing for images inside the book is generally considered part of the manuscript, and therefore the author's responsibility. This includes not only payment for the licensing costs but the administrative work of obtaining written permissions and high-resolution digital image files. Keep in mind as well that, because they will be due to the press either at delivery or immediately after, you need to plan ahead for this component. Permissions can take months to arrange. If you wait until the week after delivering the manuscript to begin working on the permissions for images, your editor will be (rightly) grumpy, or worse.

I've often been asked for ten to twenty images. I don't believe that I've ever been asked to provide fewer than five images. Licensing costs can be expensive — sometimes a thousand dollars or more per image. Five hundred dollars is pretty typical for a run of the mill historical image through a licensing agency such as Getty, although you can (and should) prioritize image searches first in some of the public image repositories that do not charge for licensing. The United States Library of Congress, for example, offers certain materials as "free to use and reuse," and I've rarely been charged to reproduce images from the collections of local historical societies, though you should be prepared, as an understood professional courtesy, to offer a complimentary copy of your published work to any institution providing *gratis* images for reproduction. But, if you must pay for the cost of licensing, the bottom line is that these are costs that come out of your advance as an author.

Before you commit to images, look to see what some actual options and costs will be. Get that image scanned while you are at the archive or research library. Ask for academic discounts on licensing. Often you will not be able to get an academic discount for use in a trade title, because it's not considered non-profit, but it is always worth asking. If you need to license through a third party such as Getty, be sure to ask for the contract rate for your publishing house. Many publishers, and nearly all Big Five publishers, have discounted contract rates, and authors with a contract can license for substantial reductions. Be sure to look carefully as well at the licensing options and their respective costs. If the price difference is minimal (and it often is), you want to request a license for retail book, interior use, world territory, all editions, to avoid having to later re-license the same image for a subsequent edition. This is especially important if you are reserving foreign rights.

Finally, consider alternatives. At one point, I needed some images for my first book, *The Widow Clicquot,* including a copy of the widow's portrait and a map of the Champagne region of France circa 1800. Because the materials were in rare books and there was only one historical portrait extant, the British Library was quoting me a shockingly high price for a copy of a scanned image of the portrait especially.

I was able to purchase an original engraved map from the 1790s, long since out of copyright protection, for less than a hundred dollars on eBay, and in an antiquarian print shop in Paris I found an original nineteenth-century engraving of the portrait from the 1880s for about four hundred dollars. Let's just say that, as an assistant professor without a lot of resources, I was able to travel from London to Paris for the weekend, buy the print (which remains displayed in my office to this day, alongside that map of Champagne), and stay in a budget hotel for about the same as the cost of licensing for the first edition — and we are now in the multiple editions. I have saved myself thousands of dollars by purchasing original art. That is not a sentence you imagine when you are an assistant professor ever someday writing, but there we are.

From here, you've done it. You've managed to sign your first trade book contract, whether you did it with the help of an agent or directly with an editor. You've hopefully learned over the course of this book how to take your first concrete steps toward not writing like an academic. Take a breather. Pop the bubbles. Torment that colleague you've never liked much with the fabulous news of your glittering success in that department meeting. When the hard work of writing begins, there are bound to be some stumbling blocks and probably some equivalent of those champagne lunches. The learning curve is real, and it's hard. You'll get there if you're determined.

In the past fifteen-plus years now that I have been doing this, writing for a large public readership has been more intellectually rewarding than anything I have done in my career. The so-called general public is smart and curious. The public sphere is more intact than we sometimes fear or imagine. The conversations are good, especially when the writing is good. Good luck, and by all means drop me an email when you get that first trade book contract: tilar@protonmail.com.

ACKNOWLEDGMENTS

I am aware as I put the final words on the manuscript that this is likely to be the last "academic" book that I will ever publish. Even in writing it, I am continuing, I see, a bit longer to attempt to straddle that line between trade and the academy. But my academic debts are not the less for it. Indeed: the contrary.

And, so, by commodious vicus of recirculation: thank you to Hazard Adams for insisting that I was tough enough to learn to be persuasive to hostile critics; to Marshall Brown for demanding that I learn where commas go and why in sentences; to Bro Adams, Ed Yeterian, and Jerry Singerman, who supported a young assistant professor in ways that only in retrospect have I understood were transformational; to Genoveva Llosa, Matt Inman, and Toni Sciarra for first showing me how to write a bestseller (and, Genoveva, thanks for those champagne lunches); to my dad, a master of effective narrative thrall, for telling us all those wild whoppers as big-eyed kids about cannibal kings, sad princesses, and souvenir golden dinner forks; to Lou Pitt, my film agent, for teaching me more about story than anyone except my dad; and to Stacey Glick, my literary agent, who, as always, makes all good things possible. A secret Colby handshake to my former students Julianna Haubner and Kat Brzozowski who have gone on, as Big Five editors, to teach me all sorts of things. Thanks to the National Endowment for the Humanities for funding a year to think hard about public scholarship, and to Peter Doughtery, without whom this book would never have seen the light of day; may the force be with you.

Closer to home, there are the little rituals, a writer's sad triennial-ish attempt to take back all those cranky mornings hunched over the computer scowling at everyone. Rob, just thanks. For all of it, with all my heart: for everything. To the boys: we survived another book! Yes, now we can go to Sointula.

Finally, thanks to Jennifer Banks, Eva Skewes, Phillip King, and the entire team at Yale University Press for shepherding this chimerical book, with all its academic ambivalence, through development and production with grace and good humor.

Index

INDEX

INDEX

INDEX

INDEX

INDEX

INDEX